# Breaking the Musashi Code

## Transcending Competition through Visionary Strategy

Matthew C. Heim, Ph.D.

Visionary Partnership Press

PUBLISHED BY
Visionary Partnership Press
PO Box 267
Sonoma CA 95476

Tel: (707) 337-3192
Fax: (707) 933-9658
www.visionarypartnership.com

This book is printed on recycled paper

ISBN-13: 978-0-9795463-0-3

1. Strategy. 2. Business. 3. Human ecology.
4. Sustainable development.

Library of Congress Control Number: 2007926361

FIRST EDITION

Back Cover Art by Timothy Helgeson

# Table of Contents

# Acknowledgments

I WOULD LIKE TO THANK Dr. Don Bushnell, Janet Garvey-Stangvik and Andreas Zynga for their wisdom and guidance, not to mention the many hours they spent carefully reviewing my initial manuscript. I would especially like to thank my wife, Kristina, for her love, caring, and most of all, patience.

# Preface

I FIRST BECAME INTERESTED IN writing this book four years ago, after years of successful strategic visioning retreats with large corporations in my consulting practice. I saw a great need for innovation in the strategic planning cycles of my corporate clients, as they continuously fought for materials, personnel and market share under the old competition-based paradigm. I noticed how these competing companies we not only growing at incremental rates, at best, but they were also contributing to the continuous depletion of our limited resources on Earth. While many expressed interest in changing, they had no idea how to go about such change.

I first began to incorporate visioning techniques into my strategic planning approach around twenty years ago, after applying similar techniques to my own business ventures. The success that I experienced in my own ventures led me to want to introduce these techniques to my corporate clients. However, this was no easy task at first. I had to first articulate, on a practical level, why visioning is effective, and how it actually worked. Being a systems scientist, this was easy for me to understand, but being able to explain it in a non scientific manner took time and several iterations before getting it right.

I have since been able to apply these same techniques to mid-sized and smaller organizations, such as entrepreneurial start-ups, museums, nonprofits and even churches. The successes that these organizations experienced in their strategic visioning, planning and management initiatives demonstrated the universal applicability of the methods discussed in this book. By success, I am referring to not only highly productive and innovative planning sessions, but more importantly, the ability to implement these plans with dramatic measurable results.

In every case, whether it be a large Fortune 500 firm or a small nonprofit, the participants are always amazed at how they are able to generate so many innovative new thoughts and ideas without having to hire an outside consulting firm to tell them what to do. In fact, many have realized since that these outside firms were doing nothing more than homogenizing their industry, by aligning them with competitive benchmarks, and never truly coming up with new breakthrough ideas. They also realized after going through the strategic visioning process that there was really nobody better equipped to do this work than their very own management team, because of their in-depth knowledge of their customers, markets, alliance partners, suppliers and, of course, products and services.

It was a mere "coincidence" that I had been brought up studying Miyamoto Musashi and his *Book of Five Rings* as a lifelong practitioner of the martial arts, while also having chosen systems science as my academic area of focus. I remember being in awe after coming to the realization that Musashi's strategic principles so closely paralleled the natural emergent principles in systems science. In fact, this was a major turning point in my life, both educationally and spiritually.

So after years of coaxing and nudging, I finally decided to sit down and write about Miyamoto Musashi and the strategic visioning process that I am presenting to you in this book. This East-meets-West strategic approach is not only unique, but also sufficiently detailed that any organization of any type or size can read it, understand it and immediately apply it. May it bring you all the success, clarity and joy that it has to those who have used it in decades past.

Matthew C. Heim, January, 2007

# Introduction:

# Toward a Visionary Strategy

DURING THE LATE SIXTEENTH and early seventeenth centuries, a legendary Samurai warrior named Miyamoto Musashi roamed the lands of feudal Japan. Although Musashi is best remembered for never having been defeated in battle, his true legacy is the comprehensive and timeless approach to strategy he developed in The Book of Five Rings. Perhaps because Musashi wrote in the context of the Samurai experience, his work was all but forgotten outside of Japan until recent breakthroughs in strategic thinking revived interest in his teachings.

When my own personal study of both Eastern and Western strategy led me to discover Musashi's work I immediately recognized the systemic nature and wide-ranging applicability of his teachings. I realized what few have learned long ago, that Musashi didn't write *The Book of Five Rings* exclusively for the Samurai. As a lifelong practitioner and teacher, he recognized the common patterns of consciousness and action that lead to strategic advantage and ultimately to a state of enlightenment. *Breaking the*

*Musashi Code* mines Musashi's Samurai metaphor for the universal principles that inform an unparalleled approach to strategic planning and management for organizations of all types and sizes.

Have you ever wondered how a few companies have been able to consistently anticipate, and even create consumer demand while outperforming their competition year after year? Isn't it funny how these companies always seem to be ahead of the market, offering their consumers the *next big thing*? Do you believe that the executives of such companies have succeeded by merely expanding on today's capabilities, today's customers, today's markets, or today's competition? If your answer to the last question is no, you're on the right path to a more visionary, creative, and enlightened state of management.

Recently, a large medical device manufacturer in Southern California hired me as a strategic advisor to help the company with its many challenges. The company was created through the merger of two organizations that had similar product lines, yet completely different processes and organizational cultures. Over the course of a few years the company lost a large amount of market share and shareholder value, and employee turnover was out of control. Not knowing exactly where to begin, the company asked me to conduct an executive visioning retreat. We gathered representatives from each area of the business, including various international business units, and introduced a type of visioning process that was quite new to the group – the Fifth Ring Strategy approach. During the visioning retreat all participants learned how to tap into their inner wisdom and intuition, as opposed to using the old brainstorming techniques they were used to. Following this powerful visioning retreat, a number of high profile initiatives were launched with great momentum and support across the company, and within one and a half years the company had completely turned itself around. Without ever having to focus on competition, their stock price went from under $5 to over $25 per share, and customers, suppliers and regulatory agencies were now viewed as partners in innovation, as opposed to challenges. Customer satisfaction ratings rose significantly, and employees were now thriving, working in highly innovative teams representing various areas of the business, continuously learning and generating new breakthrough ideas to take the company to an even higher level.

One of these breakthrough ideas was to cross industry boundaries and take a standard drug infusion device that was normally a manual stand-alone device, and turn it into an integrated software-driven system. This, in turn, let to new ideas to capture patient vital signs, drug infusion history and other vital information, and feed it back to a central server where physicians could monitor patient histories and trends from a centralized location. This new breakthrough elevated the company to the top of its market sector, and revolutionized the medical device industry as we know it.

This story may seem a bit sensational, and even somewhat unrealistic in today's marketplace, but it is, in fact, true. This company, as well as many other companies and nonprofits in similar situations learned the power of the Fifth Ring Strategy by following the transformative processes described in this book. Those who follow these processes are always amazed, not only at how they are able to transform their organizations, but more importantly, how they themselves are transformed.

When most people talk about strategy today, they tend to view it through the foggy lens of competition. Yet when an organization focuses its energy and resources primarily on competitive advantage and dominance, it will always find itself in the "heat of battle" and never experience the freedom that comes with a truly enlightened visionary state. Have you ever heard the saying, "what you put your mind to, you will eventually attract into your life?" Well, competition is no exception to the law of attraction. Musashi's teachings help us transcend these outdated competition-based paradigms, and have us focus, instead, on a higher vision. These teachings are the basis of the visioning practices I introduce in this book, which will help you set your organization apart from those still held captive by the old command-and-control way of thinking.

Rings one through four of Musashi's strategy refer to competition, but only to build a foundation for success that comes through the fifth ring. In the fifth and final ring, Musashi shifts his focus to a visionary state that transcends the competitive mindset. By using the tools and techniques I describe, your organization can enter this enlightened state, continuously reinvent itself, and ultimately transcend the competitive illusion.

At the heart of this transformation is the visioning process. Before you can begin to influence positive change within your company, you must first establish a clear guiding vision that is detached from *today's* issues and concerns. This is possible only when you enter the fifth ring and achieve what Musashi calls "Emptiness." Amazingly, Musashi was able to articulate the concept of emptiness in such a way that it can be applied to almost any type of activity, in any occupation or industry.

While many readers will be interested in learning how to transcend competition, many more will be interested in the more tangible benefits that occur by adopting the Fifth Ring Strategy approach. These include:

- Improved shareholder and stakeholder value
- Increased customer and constituent satisfaction
- Increased employee productivity and satisfaction
- A shift to a more cohesive organizational culture
- A stronger sense of social and environmental responsibility
- Improved communications and alignment within and across all organizational levels
- Creation of a work environment that is stimulating, creative, and fun

*Breaking the Musashi Code* provides a proven, integrated approach to strategic planning and management that is designed to work holistically. The approach I describe is the result of more than twenty years of research, practical experience and producing tangible results. It will help leaders of all kinds of organizations maximize vision, commitment, and alignment to their advantage, while developing a flexible, stimulating, and creative environment for employees at all levels.

Throughout this book, I often refer to *organization* as a generic, universal term. In fact, the vision-based strategic planning and management framework I present has been used successfully in organizations of all shapes and sizes, ranging from nonprofits and mom-and-pop shops to Global 500 megacorporations. In fact, it has even been used in religious institutions, communities, and even families.

Breaking the Musashi Code will provide you with the tools and techniques that will help you to recognize and strengthen individual and collective intuition within your organization, and harness it into a collective learning and development process. Building strong discipline around the key elements of vision, intention setting, and alignment at all levels of your organization will enable you and your workforce to finally transcend the competitive state and experience a lifetime of continuous innovation, profitability and excitement.

This book was not written in a linear manner, so you have many options for reading this book. If, for example, you would like to get right to the heart of the Fifth Ring Strategy approach, you may decide to go directly to Part 3 and read about the strategic visioning, planning and management process. If you would like to first learn more about Miyamoto Musashi, and *The Book of Five Rings*, I highly suggest you start with the Appendix in the back of this book. This Appendix provides a synopsis of the timeless wisdom that influenced the writing of this book, and describes the significance and relevance of each *ring* to contemporary strategic thought. You may, on the other hand, choose to follow the linear progression of this book, starting with the basics of visionary strategy in Part 1, then moving on to the foundation-forming requirements in Part 2, and ending with the Fifth Ring Strategy approach in Part 3. The choice is yours, and regardless of the path you choose, all the information you need for a holistic transformational approach is right here in this book.

# Part I

# Understanding the Basics of Visionary Strategy

PART I FOCUSES ON the foundational underpinnings of the Fifth Ring Strategy. First, I discuss some of today's more significant strategic issues in Chapter 1, and how they are the result of a continued reliance on the outmoded mechanistic models of the Industrial Age. Chapter 2 discusses the emergence of modern systems theories to show their compatibility with the wisdom that long predates them. In Chapter 3 I talk about the key managerial tools and processes that create a flexible and informative management infrastructure required for success in a rapidly changing business environment.

The ancient wisdom of *The Book of the Five Rings* has come full circle. Recent breakthroughs in systems and organization theory have made Musashi's insights, once lost to the West, available to us. Breaking the Musashi code can now free us from the organizational and managerial myths that have bound us since the beginning of the Industrial Age and prepare us to conduct business in an entirely new and better way.

# Chapter 1

# Contemporary Strategic Issues

SEVERAL HUNDRED YEARS AGO, feudalism began to give way to nation states, beginning the process that eventually produced modern organizational bureaucracy. Later, during the Industrial Age, businesses adopted the bureaucratic model in order to maintain better control over their rapidly growing organizations. Over time, the automated technologies used to manage and control large organizations became highly advanced, and they eventually gave birth to today's Information Age. Little did we know that the tools of automation, which were developed primarily for the purpose of bureaucratic control, would eventually become one of our largest and fastest growing industries.

But despite recent advances in both technology and organizational theory, nearly all organizations today continue to rely on the antiquated mechanistic models of the Industrial Age. This reliance manifests itself in the areas of organizational structure, technology, sustainability, strategy, diversity, and human capital development. Ultimately, this mechanistic reliance is what prevents organizations from achieving a higher state of visionary strategy.

## Organizational Structure

The old views of the Industrial Age, which were grounded on principles of command and control, are still alive—if not well—today. Although we can now joke about the rigid, top-down, command-and-control style of management, we are only just beginning to replace it with a management style based on a holistic understanding of how systems interact.

Recent developments in business process design and reengineering methods have demonstrated the importance of focusing on the transfer and flow of information and energy, as opposed to drawing hierarchical boxes as a means of defining organizational accountability. The old organization chart now has to either include arrows in order to ensure that communication travels an infinite path, or—better yet—give way to an organic model that depicts the way information really flows through an organization.

While organization charts can be useful in representing an organization's leadership and reporting structure, many managers and consultants still use them, erroneously, to represent and explain how their organizations function. Organizations operate through the formal and informal passing of information between various entities and individuals within and outside of their four walls. To believe that we can explain this exchange of information by means of a hierarchy chart is clearly a ridiculous notion.

In fact, even some of the more recent process-mapping

techniques used by internal and external consultants, when coupled with highly structured communication policies, can impose extreme rigidity, thereby stifling the informal communication patterns that would otherwise emerge naturally.

Mapping such patterns requires a delicate balance of structure and open-endedness. Even if it's accomplished successfully, the informal patterns of flow will shift once the participants find an easier or more meaningful way to get things done. Controlling such communication is nearly impossible. It's much more beneficial to encourage it through the use of nonrestrictive communication channels, interactive teams and more loosely defined process flows.

Implementing the integrated planning approach of Fifth Ring Strategy forces an organization to break with the old top-down-only approach. When feedback is allowed to flow back up through the ranks, command-and-control structures begin to evolve to the next level of sustainability.

## Technology

Most business leaders have finally come to realize that there is no silver-bullet technology that will leapfrog their organization ahead of their competitors. In the frenzied 1990s, organizational leaders rushed to gain competitive advantage by implementing enterprise resource planning (ERP) software systems. Then came the push toward customer relationship management (CRM) systems. Eventually, the Internet came into play. It promised much, but, for most companies, delivered very little in terms of direct bottom-line value.

Are the creators of the Internet to blame for this? How about the software companies? Clearly not. These tools are very useful and can provide significant value to almost any organization—but only if they aren't implemented to support the old business paradigms of the Industrial Age.

Managers of complex organizations must begin to think organically and take advantage of the integrating features that the new technologies offer. With or without the new technologies, if organizations don't develop strategies and processes that allow them to become more responsive and agile, whatever competitive advantage they enjoy will quickly erode from under them, and they'll never enter the realm of the fifth ring.

The dot-com era of the late 1990s was a real wake-up call for most large companies. For a time they felt seriously threatened by smaller, nimbler companies that were able to generate very innovative ideas and bring them to market in very little time. Leaders of many larger companies began to question their own inability to adapt and respond to such challenges.

In the end, most of the perceived threats proved to be of no real danger at all, and the dot-com industry began to fade. Nevertheless, some wise business leaders asked, "What if it had been true?" If a similar threat comes along with a legitimate product to offer, how will we react? Will we be prepared to compete? Will we be ready to change and evolve our products and services?

These are questions you need to ask yourself as well. If taken seriously, they can help you challenge the status quo and launch your organization into a new era of vision, innovation, and unparalleled responsiveness.

Technology is often seen as a necessary evil because of its high costs and the never-ending obsolescence that requires an organization to continually play catch-up. But if you were to view technology as a strategic enabler that helps you take your organization to its next level, you would no longer perceive it as a costly headache. By considering it an integral part of the strategic process and including technology executives in your planning process, you can turn it into a strategic opportunity bubbling with possibility.

## Sustainability

Sustainability is certainly a buzz word that has been capturing people's attention lately. In fact, in a recent survey, over two thirds of CEO's worldwide indicated that proper management of corporate responsibility is directly related to their bottom lines, and that the image associated with a company's sustainability measures will play a vital role in retaining customers and shareholders.

When most people think about sustainability, they immediately think of the elevated levels of carbon in our atmosphere, which has been causing a rapid increase in global climate change. Although most companies are concerned with these issues, they have no means, or catalyst to adopt the changes that will be necessary to make a global change in time to save our environment.

The idea of environmental sustainability goes beyond greenhouse gases. Businesses must seek out new ways of procuring, manufacturing, selling and transporting goods without causing further destruction of the earth. We must be willing to abandon food and other technologies that have proven to be hazardous to the environment and to ourselves. Customers and shareholders alike are beginning to scrutinize the products and services they buy, with a watchful eye towards a company's sustainability policies.

Social responsibility is another important element within this movement, and businesses can be the most influential in bringing about positive change in this area. Consumers and shareholders are beginning to pay attention to how and where products are being manufactured and sold, and whether or not policies are in place to ensure the safety of the employees and the communities in which they operate.

The world simply cannot sustain itself in the exploitative direction that it has been heading. There is only a limited amount of natural resources available, and only so much pollution and abuse that our planet and its occupants can take. Why can't we create products that, when finished, can be reused over and over again? Why can't disposable products be made to enrich the Earth instead of pollute it? Why is the US one of the slowest nations to get off the dime when it comes to the innovation and development of alternative energy technologies? To resolve issues like these requires that companies be equipped to take on major change initiatives and seek out new innovative solutions to meet these new demands. The Fifth Ring Strategy approach outlined in this book can be both the opportunity and the means through which such innovative changes can finally take place.

## Strategy

A strategy consists of the long-term goals and plans created or reviewed on a periodic basis (usually annually) that will enable your organization to adapt to the internal and environmental changes that would otherwise affect its performance or survivability.

The strategies that exist today in most organizations are direct derivatives of how things were just before the new strategy was developed. They are incremental steps written up in a document that cannot really be considered strategic at all. They are tactical, at best, and are typically too focused on today's markets and today's competition.

In larger organizations, strategies are still designed in a linear fashion by just a few members of the executive team as part of a five-year plan. Worse yet, some executives delegate this critical task to outsiders, relying on consultants to tell them what to do. Such plans don't take into consideration the likelihood of changes in social attitudes, deep product knowledge, employee and cultural awareness, regional legislation, alliances, and the like—all of which can render the strategy useless if not included. When unanticipated change challenges the strategy, most organizations stumble as they attempt to steer the organization onto a new course, as they lack the necessary adaptability within their structure.

After the dot-com bust and during the long recession that followed, the strategy of many companies focused on aligning their business processes to achieve maximum return on equity (ROE) and profit. They froze their information technology expenditures and sought every opportunity to squeeze budgets by reducing unnecessary spending.

Most midsized and larger companies attempted to achieve operational excellence without having an overarching vision. Each department was charged with consolidating processes, reducing headcount, and lowering costs. While this did achieve (and is still achieving) impressive cost savings at the departmental or business unit level, these companies are finding themselves left with the same organizational and information chaos as before. In fact, many of these major restructuring initiatives take place within the same leadership structures and restructuring methodologies that got them into trouble in the first place.

Business leaders too often don't assign priority to initiatives that will produce the highest value for the company. Instead, they allow business units at various levels to carry out individual agendas, leading to their competition for available resources of people, time, and money. This leads to political infighting that just confuses the customer. Consensus management, lack of empowerment, and an unwillingness to take control of the organization's destiny begin to emerge as a result. I see it every day in my line of work.

Changing such dysfunctional organizational cultures is no easy feat. Fear of accountability and change are so commonplace in some organizations that any change is incremental at best. All too often, I've heard phrases like "Oh, but that will never work here," or "It will take longer than you think because we are very consensus-driven here." If change isn't continually anticipated, people become comfortable, and all innovation and creativity eventually cease. Changing such attitudes often requires a fundamental change in an organization's culture, yet it typically takes seven to twenty years of continuous coercing to actually change the culture of an organization. Even then, there's no guarantee of the outcome. Does this sound hopeless?

Well, it isn't. Starting at the top, your organization can reinvent itself. By changing the playing field and using the right tools and methods to empower and measure effective change agents at all levels, it can transcend mediocrity. It can become an organization characterized by strong vision and continuous renewal.

Changing the playing field simply means that if your employees are used to playing baseball, you let them know that they will soon be playing football. Once they're on the new field, you give them the playing rules—the right rules—they will need to play the new game well and successfully.

It will surprise you just how quickly people become reenergized when they suddenly have to step out of their comfort zone, knowing that they will be gently guided through the new changes. While they may initially resist the change, they will quickly become motivated if you engage them, allow them to use their creative talents to improve the organization, and encourage them to play an active role in changing their own destiny. Realizing that there will be no turning back and knowing that they will have a say in their future brings out the best in most people.

This may seem to fly in the face of most change-management theory, but in real life, many organizations don't have the luxury of pampering each individual with customized interventions while the proverbial ship is rapidly sinking. Stakeholders need to take their destiny into their own hands and create new, revolutionary intentions for themselves and their workers. They do this by setting new objectives based on a common vision and holding themselves and others accountable for seeing them through. Most importantly, effective leaders will rally the workforce to stand behind them and take part in creating the future.

The traditional three- to five-year strategic plan is no longer a viable option for the simple reason that nothing is stable anymore. In today's economy, customer demands, competition, products, and markets now change from one day to the next. Ten to fifteen years ago, we would have been shocked to hear about a large company going bankrupt. Today, we hardly flinch when we read about an airline or megacorporation going under or being bought out as a result of managerial complacency, fraud, or product obsolescence. While it's very important to establish and continue to adhere to a forward-thinking vision and supporting strategies, an organization must be prepared to change its tactics at any time in response to rapidly changing market dynamics.

The integrated planning process of Fifth Ring Strategy does away with focusing too much attention on where an organization is. Instead, it transfers most of the attention to what it is becoming as the environment continuously evolves into something new and better. Once an organization becomes accustomed to this ongoing dynamic, its members will seldom want to go back to the way things were. They feel self-actualized and alive, part of an exciting process in which they participate in the creative process.

The Information Age has drastically changed the way that we do business, and the companies that are nimble, aligned, and ready for radical change are the ones now leading the way. Market followers are doomed to setting long-term goals that focus on catching up to their more nimble competitors. But guess what? These nimble market leaders are already working on new radical ideas, and before the followers can catch up, the leaders will introduce a revolutionary new product, method, or service that will again change the face of their industry.

The goal of market leaders is to fill any value void in the marketplace by creating demand based on understanding and anticipating where the customer will want to go next. As they focus, and remain focused on the much higher realm of potentiality, these market leaders compete only with themselves.

## Diversity

In the past several years, *diversity* has become another over-used, or even *abused* buzzword. Almost every large company now has a diversity committee or task force charged with keeping its hand on the demographic pulse of the organization. Its usual duty is to track ratios of the employees' ethnic backgrounds, races, genders, and countries of origin to establish hiring quotas for the upcoming year. But though members of a diversity committee can give you the latest definition of *diversity* (which tends to change frequently), they don't usually grasp its true meaning and so don't really appreciate the value of a "diverse workplace."

Yet it's a fact that the more diverse an organization's

workforce is, the more it will be able to meet reciprocal demands of an increasingly diverse marketplace. Organizations of all kinds can benefit greatly by implementing new diversity policies. But have they? The answer is clearly no—not because they don't work, but merely because they're not permitted to work. If the management team at the top of an organization (which is typically limited and not very diverse) continues to make top-down decisions without seeking input and advice from their diverse workforce, they simply cannot successfully address the needs of their diverse customers and constituents.

Organizations that learn to include the ideas of workers of all levels and skill sets in their planning activities are the ones that benefit most. Top-level managers need to realize that they cannot make such decisions in a vacuum. They need to let go of their control and enjoy the benefits that true diversity can bring.

An organization is like a symphony. The more instruments there are in it, the richer the music will be—provided the conductor knows how and when to bring each instrument into play. The conductor calls upon both the various sections and the individual instruments at the proper time. When appropriate, the oboe section does its part and the violin soloist does hers. A good conductor doesn't have to know how to play each instrument in order to achieve success. However, the better the conductor is able to bring out the best in each section and player, the more the people in the audience are likely to be pleased with the performance.

An orchestra is no different than any other organization.

When each individual member exercises his or her talent as needed—when management is prepared to leverage employee talent to maximize innovation and productivity in the most logical and effective manner—both the organization and the diverse people it serves are enriched in many ways.

Does your executive management team know of the needs of the average person on the street? Better yet, do you allow new ideas and innovative breakthroughs to percolate to the top? In many of today's large bureaucratic organizations many ideas are lost in the shuffle of everyday business. There is certainly no surefire way to ensure that your top managers are evaluating every idea before implementation, nor would such a solution be cost effective to implement. But as you will see, there are fundamental planning and management techniques that can capture the truly innovative, high-value ideas that emerge from within your organization and allow them to surface to the top planning level of the organization or its departments.

## Human Capital

Organizations today often treat their personnel as liabilities. Organizational leaders may not consciously think of their employees that way because they realize that it takes people to perform the various tasks that keep the business running. But that's precisely the problem. People viewed only as entities that carry out tasks automatically become liabilities. They always require a paycheck, which reduces an organization's cash flow. Unlike a paid-off machine, employees are never *paid in full*.

Since the early days of the Industrial Revolution, organizational theorists like Frederick Taylor have attempted to divide work into measurable segments that allow organizations to replace any worker with another who has comparable training. Even today, many process gurus believe that with a clearly documented job description and business process, any competent person can replace a worker. But the moment a leadership team adopts such ideas, they ensure that their organization's culture will shift from one of compassion to fear, from teamwork to personal survival, and from the expanded power of "we" to the limited power of "me."

The most valuable asset of any company is its people. This truism has been stated many times, but it's surprising just how many companies fail to believe or act on it. It baffles me why senior executives faced with shareholder pressures so often resort to setting goals to reduce headcount by a given percentage in order to achieve a targeted cost saving. While headcount reduction is sometimes the unfortunate fallout of a strategic initiative, it should never be the driving force.

When employees feel that their organization's culture is eroding because of ruthless decisions to reduce headcount, the best and brightest workers are usually the first to leave. These workers are the most employable and will quickly find work elsewhere, leaving an irreplaceable void in the organization. Companies that decide not to use headcount reduction to drive their strategy are often surprised at how their workforce, once awakened, contributes to their change initiative.

One of the most important attributes of effective leadership is the ability to communicate the power of positive thinking. I have facilitated many strategic planning sessions in my career, and all too often I have seen a magnificent idea emerge during the workshop, only to hear one or more of the following debilitating statements:

- "We can't afford to do that."
- "That will never work here."
- "We tried that already."
- "We don't have the people who can do that."
- "Our investors will never go for that."

These attitudes tend to bring an immediate halt to a great idea. They are death sentences not only to the idea itself, but also to all creativity and innovation. Worse yet, they spread to the managers who report directly to the leadership team, and they soon become commonplace in the organization's culture. Instead of using comments that reflect an attitude of lack and limitation, leaders should be asking:

- "How can we afford to do that?"
- "How can we make that work in our organization?"
- "Who can we get to spearhead such an initiative?"
- "How can we do it differently this time?"
- "How can we model a business case that will demonstrate the power of this idea?"

Positive thinking must be present and operating at each level of your organization in order for it to become a valuable attribute of your company's culture. There's a reason that so many best selling self-help books over the past few decades have focused on positive thinking. It works!

Remember that visionary thinking is positive thinking. Some will object that it's too touchy-feely, but since there's no pragmatic substitute, they will just need to get over it and get on board. As this becomes the characteristic attitude of your company, you will witness the immediate change in your employees' energy level as they become more and more engaged in the business and achieve unprecedented levels of self-actualization.

All human beings strive to achieve self-actualization in all areas of their lives. At work, most workers thrive when they have the opportunity to go beyond the mundane tasks of daily operations and participate in projects that tap into their creative talents. If empowered, employees at all levels will come up with innovative ideas that not only reduce cost, but also significantly increase both revenue and quality for your organization. All you need to do is to nudge them a bit, or even just offer them the opportunity to contribute.

When employees begin to be seriously viewed as sources of new ideas and growth, they suddenly become an asset, even though their salaries still have to be paid. As assets, they are accorded more dignity and respect, and in turn they produce even more. And while they're at it, they have fun and feel that they are a part of a great system.

## Resolving Today's Strategic Issues

The integrated planning process of the Fifth Ring Strategy is designed specifically to overcome today's strategic issues, not by fighting them or resolving them one by one, but by making them completely irrelevant by transcending them.

Often, a select few at the top of an organization set strategic objectives, only to see them fall into the great abyss that lies between strategic planning and implementation. All too often, those few at the top do their planning in isolation while an inside or outside coordinator pulls the plans together into a set of competing plans based on high-level budget allocations.

Instead of this scenario, imagine establishing strategic objectives with the inputs of all key stakeholders and then unleashing the innovative power of hundreds, thousands, or even tens of thousands of people to achieve them. If you aren't prepared to let go of control and step outside your comfort zone, you might as well stop reading this book right now. If, on the other hand, you want to unleash this transformative power in your organization, keep reading. By embracing the management concepts of continuous empowerment, accountability and transformation, you'll see your organization come to life in ways you never could have imagined.

There is quite literally no time like the present. Recent breakthroughs in systems science based on nonlinear thinking have made it possible to break the Musashi code. Using Musashi's strategic principles, it's now possible for you to transform your organization.

# Chapter 2

# Nonlinear Thinking

WHILE SYSTEMS THINKING IS nothing new, until very recently formal systems science was ridiculed for its lack of ability to measure, predict, control, and repeat precise experimental outcomes. Lately, however, breakthroughs based on nonlinear thinking have begun to open our minds to new ideas about the scientific approach. The sudden realization that nothing is really as it seems, coupled with the fact that everything is connected at the subatomic level, has threatened the very existence of Western scientific institutions that have built their reputations and legitimacy on linear thinking.

## Empirical Science

The major premise of Newtonian-Cartesian science is that the universe works in a stable and predictable way, just like the mechanics of a clock, and that the only way to understand it scientifically is to understand each individual part. Empirical science breaks down each identifiable part to a lower level of detail, subjects it to rigorous quantitative modeling, and then attempts to apply the findings to areas not yet explored.

For almost three hundred years the scientific community believed that the only way to understand and control the *whole* was to break it down and understand its individual parts. The Scientific Revolution closed the door on holistic thinking in areas that weren't subject to the scientific method, such as organizational dynamics, psychology, and the social sciences in general. Had it not been for a few courageous thinkers throughout this long period, ideas based on integrated, holistic thought could have been completely forgotten, for such ideas were considered either philosophical or ecclesiastical and thus totally at odds with scientific discipline. Only with new discoveries in quantum, relativity, and systems theories have we come to realize that reality is more unpredictable and nonlinear than we could ever have imagined. If we cannot tame it, or beat it into submission, then we'd better understand it and learn to work with it.

While empirical scientific inquiry has led to major breakthroughs in science, engineering, and medicine, it has also resulted in a widespread belief that it is the *only* viable method of scientific inquiry. These old beliefs may have worked well in the early days of the Industrial Age, but they are no longer exclusively sustainable in today's complex environment.

Today we still don't fully understand the complexity and integrated nature of human consciousness, and as we add more people to the mix of today's growing organizational environments, the complexity increases significantly.

However, most of us have come to realize that experimental inquiry is seldom applicable in cases involving large-scale human endeavor. We have learned to accept its complexity and lack of predictability and to create more experiential ways of understanding it.

If we want to truly understand human and organizational dynamics, we must take into consideration the synergies and relationships that are created through rapidly changing and evolving interactions. As we are trying to understand the parts, we must also study the relationships between them that make things work as they do.

The recent acceptance of systems science has already had some impact on the way we manage our organizations, but the ripple effect has been a slow one. Much of existing management theory still rests on the scientific theories developed by Sir Isaac Newton and Rene Descartes nearly three hundred years ago.

Understanding the underlying principles of systems theory and quantum mechanics is essential for organizations operating in today's ever-changing marketplace, and systems thinking plays a vital role in achieving the Fifth Ring Strategy.

## Open Systems

In the 1920s, Ludwig von Bertalanffy developed the first formal theoretical framework pertaining to open systems. By studying the principles of thermodynamics, he came to understand how a living system, if closed to the outside world, ends up in a state of equilibrium that eventually destroys it. An open system, on the other hand, functions in a state of "flowing balance." Energy from the outside continuously replenishes the system, reinforcing its ability to survive while sustaining the dynamically balanced nature that gives it its identity.

When we apply Bertalanffy's theory of flowing balance to organizations, we begin to understand the importance of an open-systems design in developing long-term strategic plans. An organization needs external entities such as customers, suppliers, stakeholders, and strategic partners to improve its market access and visibility. While managers have long understood the need to maintain formal relationships with entities outside the four walls of their organization, they seldom include them as symbiotic partners in their organizational processes. Many departmental, regional, and divisional managers even today fail to view their own areas of responsibility as an integral part of the entire organization, simply because they haven't been shown the big picture.

Once you see both external and internal entities as integral parts of your organization, you'll begin to recognize new opportunities for creating win-win business scenarios by enhancing interactions and relationships. These relationships are truly symbiotic, as an organization, or even one of its departments, cannot survive without them. Managers need to include these entities in their strategic thinking as they consider new ways to grow and improve their organization.

## Cybernetics

Cybernetics is a systems-based theoretical construct developed in an attempt to map out the systemic principles of the human mind and other natural phenomena. The study of cybernetics has increased our understanding of three crucial aspects of living systems:

- the significance of feedback
- the ability of systems to self-regulate
- the ability of systems to self-organize

A simple example of a cybernetic system is that of a thermostat hooked up to a heater. The thermostat provides feedback by letting the heater know when the temperature drops below the indicated setting. Then the heater automatically self-regulates through its control unit, which turns on the heater to return the temperature to the desired setting. A more complex human example would be driving an automobile. When people drive, they get feedback by monitoring the car's instruments and outside road conditions. As things change, they make adjustments to keep the car on the road and arrive safely at their destination.

While these two examples demonstrate cybernetic systems, they don't go beyond self-regulation. Using an organization as an example of a system adds more complexity to the situation. A typical organization provides feedback through performance reports, usually to let its managers know that things are going well and that they don't need to change anything. When a report indicates that desired performance measures aren't being achieved in a particular department, the manager makes slight modifications to increase productivity or output. While this is an effective means of self-regulation at the departmental or even divisional level, it doesn't provide a means for self-organization when necessary. In fact, in most cases self-organization isn't even considered an option.

It's unfortunate that most long-term organizational strategies stop at self-regulation. According to today's standards, when they achieve this, their strategy is considered "best-in-class." So-called best-in-class companies roll out their strategic plans using self-regulating tools like key performance indicators, metrics, and scorecards built on formal feedback mechanisms. But only rarely do they progress to the next level and formally recognize the need for self-organization in their performance measurement systems. Furthermore, they almost never have a process in place that enables them to rapidly adapt to outside stimuli. This would require a fluid mindset or culture that many organizations today don't possess.

Every day we hear about organizations that are restructuring in one way or another. In fact, restructuring reactionary companies just happens to have created a booming consulting industry. When a company decides to reorganize, reengineer, or simply change, it's usually because of competitive or shareholder pressure. If reorganization were viewed as an inevitable, ongoing part of organizational life, more companies would include the concept of self-organization in their strategic plans, organizational processes, and budgets.

In order to embrace such a proactive form of self-organization, you first have to embrace strategic planning and management methods that continuously draw your attention to what *is becoming*, and not simply to what *is*. A fluid mindset is the heart and soul of a vision-based Fifth Ring Strategy process in Part 3 of this book.

## Autopoiesis

Autopoiesis (also known as Santiago Theory) is the theory that is focused primarily on self-producing systems. Although a cell receives food and energy from sources outside itself, its reproduction occurs through an organizational process that is completely self-contained within the structure of the cell itself. This breakthrough in our understanding of cellular development and of self-producing systems in general has had a major impact on our understanding of the development of the nervous system, human consciousness, and the unique human attribute, language.

By using the idea of autopoiesis as a metaphoric lens for viewing human organizations, you can begin to see how the unique collective mindset, interpretation of events, and even language-based nuances of your organization have developed. By providing a structure conducive to autopoietic development, an organization can create the communication channels, cohesive alignment, and collective consciousness that will enable it to respond more rapidly and effectively to external influences such as competitive, market, and shareholder pressures.

Such an organization isn't likely to disenfranchise its members, and in turn its members will feel a stronger sense of belonging. When the need arises for rapid change, your organization is more likely to move as a single, unified organism and achieve what you set out to do in a coordinated fashion. Organizations that don't have the same sense of commonality and alignment often struggle when the time comes for a major change.

## Chaos and Complexity

Chaos theory was formalized in the 1960s. Its roots, however, lie in the disciplines of systems theory discussed previously. All of these theories shed light on the principle of self-organization and the emergence of new systems out of existing ones. However, the nonlinear mathematical models needed for calculating, and hence fully understanding, these phenomena came into existence only with the development of chaos theory.

While experimenting with mathematical models, scientists and mathematicians determined not only how patterns naturally emerge out of chaotic, or perceived random events, but also approximately at what point they will occur based on a system's thresholds for tolerating disturbances from the outside. A system that is subject to an increasing level of external disturbance will eventually either bifurcate into a new order or else begin to dissipate.

While the continuous bifurcation, or unfolding, of new systems could be tested on simple systems that provided simple mathematical parameters for calculation, chaos theory couldn't be consistently applied to more complex human and social systems. Yet even though their ability to measure such systems quantitatively was limited, systems scientists were certain that the principles of chaos also applied to them. This assumption gave birth to the new socially oriented theory of complexity.

When applied to the development of human organizations, complexity theory demolishes the notion that prediction and control are possible if we can just figure out the right formula. We have never found this formula. Instead, what we've seen is one management strategy after another promising to lead organizations into the promised land of total prediction and control, yet all falling back into the wilderness before they reach their goal. Frighteningly enough, some people actually still believe that total prediction and control is possible in complex organizations. Yet we can begin to influence change only when we accept that change is inevitable, and the sources of change are infinite.

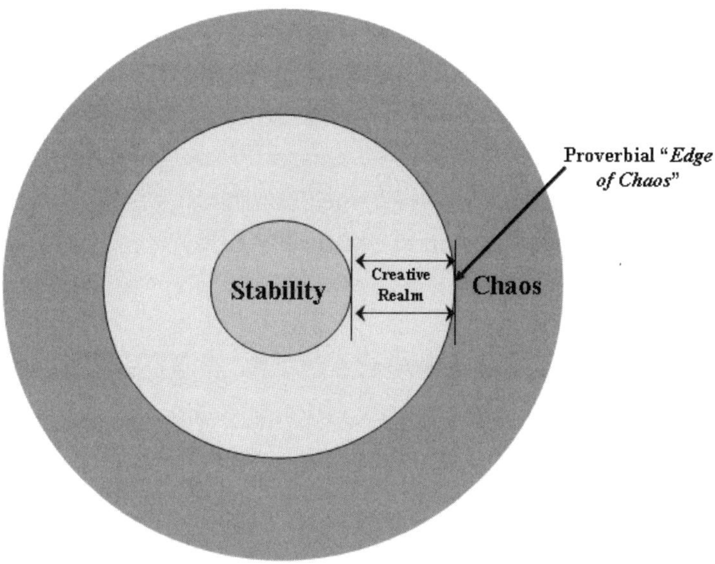


Figure 1. Balance on the "Edge of Chaos"

Managing complexity for maximum benefit requires a keen sense of balance between *legitimate* and *shadow* systems. A legitimate system consists of the formal vision, structure, and policies that create order within an organization. If too rigid, a legitimate system can stifle the free flow of thought, communication, and creativity, in which case the organization ends up in a stable state, or stasis. If too relaxed, the system will lose its common vision and will eventually end up in a state of unguided chaos (see figure 1).

The shadow system, better known as the company *grapevine*, consists of the informal networks that form outside the formal boundaries set by the legitimate system. This is a natural system that exists in every organization, and it can be very beneficial during times of change. It would be futile, and perhaps even dangerous, to try to suppress the shadow system or to try to prevent it from challenging the status quo. However, it's equally dangerous to allow it to completely disregard the legitimate system, as this will eventually lead to the ultimate demise of the shared vision as different entities attempt to carry out their own agendas.

The key is to strike the right balance between order and creativity, and this takes experience, wisdom, and a clear understanding of your organization's mission and culture. A good balance between the legitimate and shadow systems will allow you to harness raw talent and creativity and guide your organization toward sustainability and overall success as it achieves its vision. The integrated steps of the Fifth Ring Strategy provide the means for striking this important balance.

## Quantum Mechanics

While quantum mechanics isn't actually considered a systems-based theory, it has had a major impact on understanding human consciousness and the significant part it plays in determining the design of the world in which we live and operate.

The quantum principle of *uncertainty* dictates that an experiment cannot be conducted without the observer influencing the outcome in some way. This was the conclusion of several experiments designed to determine whether light consisted of waves or particles. The surprising answer to this question was that *it depends*. When the scientist was watching the light during the experiment, the light would collapse from a wave state into a particle, or matter. When the scientist wasn't watching the light, recordings show that the light would remain a wave, or non-matter.

Similar studies have shown that atoms consist of space occupied by light forms that transition from waves to particles and back again. They have also shown that an atom's subcomponents lack commitment to it. They fire from one atom to another, creating a dynamic relationship between atoms and their subcomponents that result in an energy field. These experiments shed light (no pun intended) on the possibilities that human consciousness can alter, or even manifest, matter.

Quantum mechanics shows us that we, like all things, are formations within a universal field of flowing energy that are connected at the subatomic level and held together by consciousness and intention. Because of this breakthrough, we are now beginning to develop new paradigms based on the concepts of quantum possibility and conscious intention, such as the law of attraction. These paradigms are just now beginning to influence social and organizational theory, and the organizations on the leading edge are clearly reaping the benefits.

Since the dramatic breakthroughs in thought spawned by the discoveries of new scientific theory, we have begun to witness the slow reemergence of systems thinking in a variety of disciplines. Within the short period of time in which systems thinking has become widely accepted, we have begun to see dramatic progress in areas where researchers are using integrated, cross-disciplinary methods to acquire new knowledge.

Although some highly reputable academic and scientific institutions still refuse to open up and accept the new non-empirical, qualitative scientific methods, this has only temporarily delayed the development of an integrated method for attaining strategic success. In the spirit of a truly integrated approach, we cannot ignore the golden nuggets that Miyamoto Musashi has provided us (see Appendix). While his principles may not be considered "scientific," they are based on and validated by centuries of cumulative intuition, knowledge, and experience—also known as *wisdom*.

Systems thinking provides the means to understand and optimize the organic flow of information throughout our organizations and into those of our customers, constituents, suppliers, and strategic partners. Understanding systems and quantum theory shows us how important it is to know both what exists and what does not yet exist in your organization, and how our intentions can influence an outcome. It should also help you see how you can harness the power of human consciousness and intention to accomplish what you once considered unachievable goals. When you direct your attention to your organization's ever-emerging patterns, you will be less likely to get caught up in the minutiae of little or no strategic value that will otherwise fill your mind and consume an inordinate amount of your time.

While understanding the impact of systems and quantum theories on your organization is mostly a matter of science, applying the insights derived from them is chiefly an art. Throughout the rest of this book, I'll provide you with the key steps necessary in allowing these systemic principles to unfold in your organization, as they are absolutely crucial to the successful implementation of the Fifth Ring Strategy.

## Chapter 3

# Laying a Firm Foundation

ORGANIZATIONS THAT EXPECT TO survive in today's market-driven economy must master the art of balance. They must focus on continuous adaptability and self-renewal while not losing sight of traditional knowledge and wisdom. The fate of the dot-coms provides us with a recent and telling example of companies that have failed to achieve this balance.

## The Dot-Com Debacle

Beginning in the late 1980s, companies of all kinds worldwide became willing to sacrifice and even cannibalize themselves to gain some kind of competitive advantage. New forms of innovative competition began to emerge from a fleet of start-ups that were giving their much larger counterparts a run for their money. Smaller and nimbler, they weren't afraid to ravage their product-based or service-based revenue streams to capture the holy grail of customer loyalty from a new marketing channel that was beginning to catch on—the dot-com.

Investors from around the world began to throw money at these daring new companies that were promising to usher in a new age. Although it had taken several hundred years to shift from the Industrial Age to the Information Age, technology innovation was now doubling every eighteen months, and it was beginning to look as if Moore's Law was going to catapult us into the Internet Age within a fraction of that time.

But along with the new millennium came a big surprise—the new dot-com companies failed to deliver. It looked as if the Internet wasn't going to revolutionize the way we did business after all. It seemed that many people, while not afraid to shop over the Internet, much preferred the personal touch and feel of shopping in a store, or a personal handshake. While the technology could change the way in which we do business, it couldn't change the culture quite so fast.

Once the sleeping giants awakened from the bad dream in which they saw themselves threatened by small dot-com intruders, they adopted the new capabilities the Internet provided, and linked them to the legitimate products and services that the public was used to. Through savvy intranet and extranet solutions, larger businesses began to build online functions for their customers, constituents, suppliers, and personnel.

Once they had proved that they could be as nimble as their dot-com counterparts, they began to compete amongst themselves for market share in the new territory offered by the Internet. From that point on, there was no turning back. Larger companies became used to changing their tactics on a regular basis in their attempt to dominate their markets, and the Internet became just another tool for them. But these companies never mastered the ability to change as quickly at the strategic level, and that caused much undue waste through internal competition for resources.

Temporary start-stop programs caused additional confusion and turnover at all levels. A company usually allocates resources to these programs after it develops a three-to-five-year strategy. Once a program has been initiated, deployed, and completed, those resources return to their operational functions until the next strategy or program dictates another change. Such programs pull workers at all levels from their perceived state of *stability*, or operational state, and push them into a strategic program that is project-oriented and milestone-driven. They are then expected to deliver on a new process or system while maintaining their old operational role in the company.

Because most companies wait until the need is urgent before they decide to change, the transition between the operational state and the program state is at best rocky and contentious. Those involved in such program activities are usually the best and brightest individuals in the company, but they eventually become confused as a result of the conflicting priorities of constant start-stop activities. Launching new programs every few years causes even the best employees and managers to feel uneasy, and eventually they burn out.

A company with an organic structure, on the other hand, is able to adapt to external forces in a more fluid manner and to rapidly and successfully implement needed change while avoiding employee burnout. It doesn't have to wait until the next strategic plan is completed to be able to act. This requires balanced interaction among organizational structure, business process, and strategic process and programs.

During the last two decades, we have increased our ability to create more fluid organizational structures and business processes, but we are still missing the key driver in the mix—strategic process. Strategic process is different from business process in that it doesn't define regular recurring cycles of business activity. Rather, it's a meta-cycle that continuously collects, processes, and redistributes new information throughout the organization, keeping it in a continual state of strategic awareness, fluctuation, and change. Simply put, the old notion of the three-to-five-year strategy has had its day.

The rapidity with which an organization can change to adapt to external or environmental situations depends on a number of structural and organizational factors. Although changing your organization's culture takes years, there are some catalysts that can immediately influence the behaviors of the individuals and groups that make it up. If you put these catalysts in place and properly manage them, the desired behavior will slowly become engrained in your organization's culture.

While it would take an entire book to adequately explain the development of an effective organization model, I will explain briefly the ten structural and activity-based elements your organization needs to support the Fifth Ring Strategy—a planning and management process that drives continuous, organic change.

## 1. A Simple Vision

Having a simple vision is the basis upon which all the other elements rest. Your organization must first of all have a timeless, sustainable vision statement that keeps it focused on continuously developing and improving itself. Strategies are intended to keep an organization moving in the right direction, and the vision determines that right direction.

The next key ingredient for strategic success is alignment. Without the proper alignment between the visionary body and action-oriented entities of the organization, the strategic intent may cause confusion, or if results aren't achieved within a reasonable period of time, even apathy.

I often encounter an organization that's obviously out of sync, with little to no alignment across all entities, only to find that it does in fact have a sound vision and a reasonable strategy. After blowing the dust off the strategy documents—usually being used as doorstops at this point—I discover that the problem is that the company isn't horizontally and vertically aligned.

## 2. Horizontal Alignment

The most effective corporate or business strategy is the result of the entire senior leadership team working together in a joint planning session. If your senior management team hasn't collectively created your organization's strategy, it must intentionally align itself with the current vision and strategies. This can be done in a strategy workshop in which the vision is revisited to ensure that the management team is fully aligned behind it before it develops a new strategy.

Once horizontal alignment has been achieved, the management team is ready to take it to the next level (literally) by means of vertical alignment.

## 3. Vertical Alignment

Once the strategic plan has been developed or revised, it's up to the leadership team to ensure that it's effectively communicated to the lower levels of the organization. This is so vital to the success of the Fifth Ring Strategy that it must be mandated and guided via a comprehensive communication plan. The components of the new strategy must be passed on to midlevel managers so that they in turn can convey the message to those who report directly to them. This ensures that all employees of the organization not only receive the message, but also know what they need to do to make the strategy successful. If the strategy isn't passed through the organization from top to bottom, it most likely will never be executed.

## 4. Employee Levels

Organizations with only a few management levels are much more likely to achieve change than those whose management tiers are steeply stacked. Clearly, structure cannot be done away with completely, as that could lead to chaos. The goal is to strike the right balance between structure and flow. There must be enough structure to maintain accountability, but not so much that it stifles the creative flow of the workforce. Non managerial positions should be designed without authority structure in mind, and management titles should be vaguely defined to allow for flexibility and empowerment.

This vague description of job titles is also conducive to the development of teams, which are a necessary part of an organic organization. For example, an *analyst* can be a worker assigned to any number of tasks while still having the empowerment that comes with a title signifying a professional position. The title *accounts payable clerk*, on the other hand, limits a worker to one task and neither encourages adaptation, nor provides a sense of professionalism or empowerment to do other things necessary for the organization to change and adapt as needed.

## 5. Bottom-Up Feedback

Just as information needs to flow from top to bottom, information needs to flow from the bottom to the top. This information is different in nature, but it's just as vital to your organization's ability to continuously adapt and change as needed. As your employees work toward guided change, they will encounter unanticipated obstacles, develop creative solutions, and receive both solicited and unsolicited feedback from customers, competitors, suppliers, and other third-party partners. This kind of information is clearly very important, but it is rarely captured and communicated up through the ranks by way of a formal communication process.

This is a significant point of breakdown that differentiates an organic organization from a mechanistic one. Simple, routine status meetings or standing meetings should collect daily, weekly, monthly, and quarterly feedback pertaining to new ideas, obstacles, results, and external changes. This feedback is then channeled back up through the ranks. Each responsible executive reviews it and proposes strategic changes as necessary.

Expectations must be set at each level of management so that bottom-up feedback becomes a formal part of each relationship between managers and the employees who report directly to them.

## 6. Achievement-Based Incentives

Whenever I evaluate a company's strategic planning and management process, one of my first stops is the human resources department. I can usually tell just how serious a company is about change by interviewing the department head. If the human resources department is involved in the company's strategic planning sessions and has a process by which they adapt their resource plans and reward systems to support newly developed strategies, I start to get that warm and fuzzy feeling. If, on the other hand, they aren't involved in the planning process, but just focus on the day-to-day operational tasks of collecting and evaluating performance reviews and administering benefits, I know that I have my work cut out for me.

If you want your organization to change, ultimately it's the people working there who will allow the change to occur. If these people are not effectively motivated, change is likely not to occur. The human resources department plays a critical role in the success of the Fifth Ring Strategy by driving the behaviors that ultimately lead to the desired change.

For example, the sales bonuses and commissions of one insurance company I consulted supported their salespeople's ability to sell more of policy A, when in fact, policy A was being phased out in favor of policy B. In the meantime, these key sales employees were working several extra hours each day on a strategic project to develop a process that would enable them to sell policy B more effectively.

This company's salespeople weren't given additional incentives either to sell more Policy B or to build the new process to support sales of it. On the other hand, they had several years' experience at selling policy A and were in fact making more money through commissions by sticking to the status quo. Do you see where I'm going with this? That's right. Even though policy B was the product targeted to carry this company into the next decade, there was no incentive to change.

Human resource departments can make a major contribution to strategic achievement. As new strategies are created in the visioning and planning process, they interface with the human resource planning process through the direct participation of executives from human resources. Understanding the direction in which the organization desires to change, the human resources department adapts every employee-touching process to foster the new direction by linking human resources with organizational strategies. Such strategic process adaptations include:

- Seeking new hires with skills and experience that complement the new strategic direction
- Modifying employee administrative procedures to support the new requirements

- Adapting employee performance criteria to assess and motivate employees in a desirable direction of personal and professional growth
- Attaching compensation and select benefits with performance that supports the new strategy
- Providing incentives and rewards that motivate employees to generate creative and innovative new ideas in support of the strategy

Figure 2 displays the optimum flow of strategic information and feedback between the higher strategic planning process and human resources:

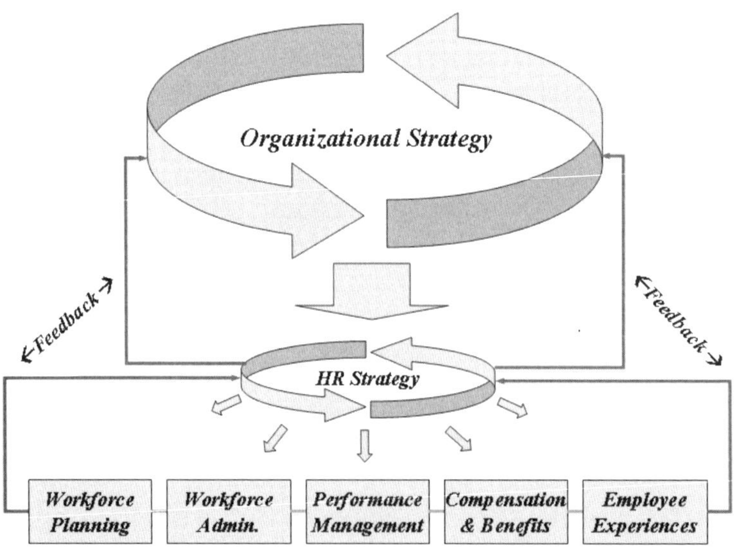


Figure 2: Strategic and Human Resources Planning Interface

## 7. Vision-Oriented Job Descriptions

Job descriptions are the primary way that new employees come to understand what a company expects from them. Therefore, they are the place to begin to instill your company's expectations regarding its vision and the role new employees will play as a part of the greater whole. Task-oriented job descriptions will lead to task-oriented work. And employees who engage in task-oriented work without any understanding of why they are doing what they are doing will be less inclined to think creatively.

When a situation arises that requires problem solving, the first thing they will do is aggravate the problem instead of attempting to understand it. Why? Because it's not in their job descriptions. If, on the other hand, employees' job descriptions are general, adaptable, and oriented toward generating creative solutions and regular team participation, they will be more likely to take a stab at solving the problem.

If employees' job descriptions are also tied to the company's vision, they will be more likely to come up with creative solutions conducive to attaining it. This also makes managing employees much easier. Managers are more likely to empower their workers to make decisions if they feel assured that they will act on behalf of the company's vision.

## 8. Flexible, Aligned Metrics

Employee rewards are a crucial part of guiding your organization in the desired direction. Equally important are the metrics, or the measures by which you evaluate your employees and managers. Metrics provide a quantitative way to measure the extent to which individual employees, teams, and departments have accomplished what you expect of them. Rewards are then allocated to those that have achieved their pre-established goals. Metrics should be established at all levels of your organization based on what are known as Key Performance Indicators, or KPIs.

Simply put, these are measures by which an organization's key shareholders evaluate it to determine whether or not they will continue to support, or invest in it. KPIs are set at the highest level of the organization and are designed to maximize shareholder or constituent value.

In public companies, depending on the industry, KPIs can represent return on equity (ROE), profitability, or various productivity ratios. In nonprofits, KPIs can take the form of the number of people assisted or the percentage of income directly attributed to its mission-related services. If, for example, profitability is directly impacted by cost of goods sold, each area contributing to cost of goods sold (materials, production costs, outsourcing, and so on) would require its own cost thresholds and would need to be monitored through an ongoing management and reporting process.

Once the KPIs have been established and quantitative goals set, each functional area or business process must be assessed for its potential to directly contribute to the success of each KPI. Metrics are most effective when they can be logically linked in a treelike fashion throughout the organization to the highest-level KPI. If directly tied to rewards, they can then be effectively used to increase productivity or decrease waste.

Finally, and most importantly, metrics should remain flexible and adaptable. Each time the organization's strategy changes, so should the metrics in order to motivate and drive desirable outcomes in performance, and align reporting procedures with the new strategy.

## 9. Horizontal Consultation and Networking

In mechanistic organizations where change is either avoided or simply not achievable, there are often strict command-and-control communications that take the form of authoritative commands or top-down decisions that are imposed on lower levels. In contrast, the communication channels of organic organizations are oriented horizontally. Peers communicate more frequently in a less formal, network style. When people at any level need information, they don't feel compelled to wait until they are told what to do. They simply go get the information, make the decision, and take action accordingly.

There are a few cases where the more rigid, command-and-control communication style is warranted, such as in the military or in a highly regulated industry setting like a nuclear power plant. In most industries, however, fluidity and adaptability are more efficacious for success. In fluid companies, interactive teams begin to replace hierarchies; consultation begins to take the place of authority and command; and cooperation, advice giving, and contribution to the mission become more highly valued than command, control, and obedience.

As these changes take place, workers at all levels feel

a sense of connectedness and belonging. This goes a long way in industries where turnover costs are high and good people are hard to come by.

## 10. Balancing New Ideas with Institutional Wisdom

The lack of legitimate value-producing products and services of the dot-com companies is the perfect segue to my next topic. While those young companies were generating a great many creative new ideas, they were often ignoring the macroeconomic trends that left them vulnerable to the fluctuations of product and sector valuation in the stock market. They saw the massive investments in their companies as the way to either get rich quick or to buy companies that didn't match their strategic focus. They failed to take into account the two major factors that eventually led to the demise of all but the strongest dot-coms—product complacency and the long-term investment patterns of investors. Striking a balance between generating fresh ideas and applying institutional wisdom would have greatly benefited the dot-com industry.

The fate of many defense industry companies is a good example of the exact opposite of what happened to the dot-com industry. Well-connected ex-military officers built post-military careers by starting overseas firms working for the US military under various defense contracts. These firms were successful until the end of the Cold War, when the first Bush administration began to close down military bases and terminate the associated contracts.

Many of these firms were unable to make the switch

to civilian contracts or those in other government sectors because they relied almost exclusively on personnel highly experienced in only the area of the contract. They didn't allow for cross-pollination by young workers or workers from nonmilitary industries who could have given them new ideas and insights as they transitioned from the military to other sectors. The people in the good-old-boy's network, while very knowledgeable in their respective job functions, rejected all but retired military personnel. The few non-retired military workers who were brought in weren't allowed to participate in a way that could have saved these companies from their demise.

When the dot-com era of the late 1990s came to a screeching halt, we all saw how ignoring wisdom—a careful mix of intelligence, intuition, and experience—can backfire on an entire global economy. Only those who had experienced the unpredictable, yet inevitable ebb and flow of economic cycles over several bear and bull markets knew that the over-valued, product-shy, dot-com driven economy couldn't last forever.

The majority of those young men and women who failed to realize the inevitable had never in their entire careers experienced a down economy. Therefore, they lacked the experience and wisdom they needed to anticipate the cyclic decline. How were they to know that the boom would ultimately bust and that the megacorporations they had scared so badly would ultimately wake up and begin to generate some of their own innovative ideas? The patience of those wise leaders has slowly paid off, and as the markets have begun to rise once again, so has a new business paradigm that enables large organizations to respond more quickly and effectively to their customers, alliance partners, and stakeholders.

However, the strategic issues still remain, even for these time-tested survivors. While they were able to develop a high state of responsiveness at the operational and tactical levels, they still struggle to achieve the fully integrated, responsive, and adaptable strategic capability that could potentially prevent events like the dot-com bust from ever happening again. Until such multilevel alignment is achieved, organizations will struggle to meet continuous competitive demands.

Balance is a recurring theme in Fifth Ring Strategy. There's a need for balance between structure and free-flowing communication, between top-down and bottom-up communication, between horizontal and vertical alignment, between clear task definition and open-endedness, and between traditional wisdom and new ideas. In order to effectively manage the balancing act necessary to keep an organization on the cutting edge, you must be able to recognize the various patterns that emerge out of your organization and be able to understand their relevance to managing complex environments.

If you're serious about adopting the model of Fifth Ring Strategy for your company, you have to consider getting rid of any highly segmented command-and-control structures. Maintaining a linear strategic planning process and mechanistic organization model while trying to change and adapt to the marketplace is like trying to cross the ocean in a sailboat with its rudder locked in one position. You will always be in conflict with the elements.

This means that the organizational structure and processes of a company must always be in alignment with the end—the vision—and your company must be prepared to adapt quickly to unanticipated change. Once the end and means are in sync, it will experience an unprecedented and unforeseen level of creativity, synergy, adaptability, and success.

To guide your organization through times of change, you'll need seasoned leaders who possess both an understanding of organizational dynamics and the experience and wisdom needed to make wise decisions. They will need to be able to clearly articulate the vision, create horizontal alignment among their executive teams, and then achieve vertical alignment down through the ranks by reaching every member of the organization. A careful balancing of useful structure and the allowance of creative and interactive play is the key to the long-term survivability of any organization.

Once there is horizontal and vertical alignment around a clear vision, your executive team can focus on the strategic issues and challenges at hand, trusting that the entire organization is working diligently, creatively, and organically to achieve the common goals of your organization.

Now that you know the basic elements that need to be in place to support the Fifth Ring Strategy, it's time to revisit Musashi's first four rings to show you exactly how you can effectively apply his strategic principles to your organization.

# Part II

# Creating an Infrastructure for Fifth Ring Strategy

In Part II, the focus shifts from theory to the practical knowledge you'll need to steer your organization toward a perpetual state of excellence. This information will enable you to create an environment conducive to implementing the Fifth Ring Strategy. Putting in place the developmental tools and processes I describe is absolutely essential if you want to sustain strategic excellence through a lifecycle of continuous change and growth.

In the chapters that follow, I discuss Musashi's first four rings (see Appendix) to show you how you can apply his strategic principles effectively in today's market-driven environment. Keep in mind that these chapters primarily address the developmental and competitive stages of an organization. A start-up will find the recommendations very appropriate for the inception phase, while an existing organization can use them to rebuild a solid foundation upon which it can prosper.

Much of the information in these chapters is oriented toward larger, more complex organizations. Therefore, I have included tips at the end of chapters 4 through 7 to provide specific guidelines that will help smaller organizations and nonprofits implement the principles of the first four rings.

## Chapter 4

# Earth: Grounding the Vision

TRUE STRATEGY IS A direct derivative of vision. Many companies I've advised over the years have tried to use financial goals as a starting point for their strategies, and even their visions. This is a mistake. While financial goal setting, accounting, and reporting play a vital role in the life of any organization, they don't belong at the top of the strategic pyramid.

Introducing visions based on financial measures can limit an organization by restricting the creativity of participants who can't buy into a profit-driven vision. On the other hand, having a strong vision statement, a clear mission statement, and a statement of sound core values can capture the allegiance of all employees in every department and motivate them to do their best to contribute to the company's overarching vision. Along with knowledge and intelligence, these statements of principle will ground your vision and prepare the way for your organization's success.

## The Vision Statement

Vision is a way of establishing a collective intention. Without intention, there's no guarantee you'll achieve a desired outcome. That's why a vision statement must be in place before any other aspect of strategic planning can begin.

Without vision, your organization is most likely to slip into chaos. The various entities within it will begin to compete with each other for available resources, and key decisions will be based solely on the interest of each individual entity or person making that decision (see figure 3).

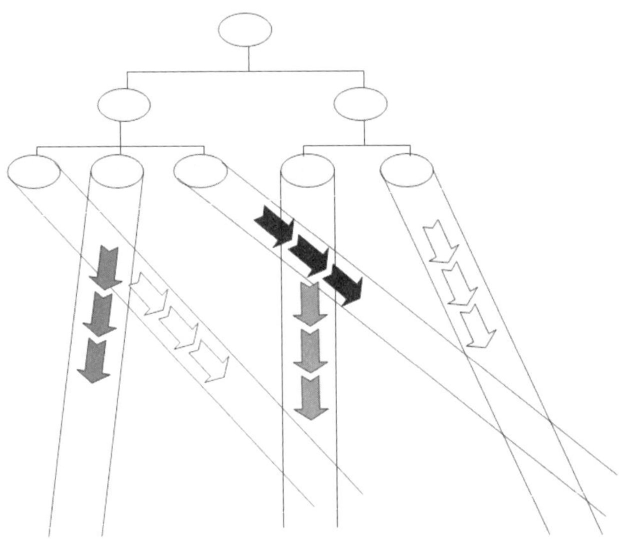

Figure 3. Organization Without a Common Vision

The ovals in the diagram depicted in figure 3 represent the managerial nodes within your organization. In the absence of a unified vision, alignment exists only at the division or department level, giving the organization a look and feel completely devoid of vision or strategy.

Figure 4 shows an organizational model with a common vision. In this case, the visionary component serves as a conduit between shareholders, customers, markets, and organizational leadership, thereby creating a unified vision. In turn, departments and division leaders, driven by a set of common intentions, augment the vision with their own aligned requirements. Finally, the lower levels of the organization (those actually carrying out the vision) provide ongoing feedback that allows your organization to adapt quickly and organically to ongoing market challenges.

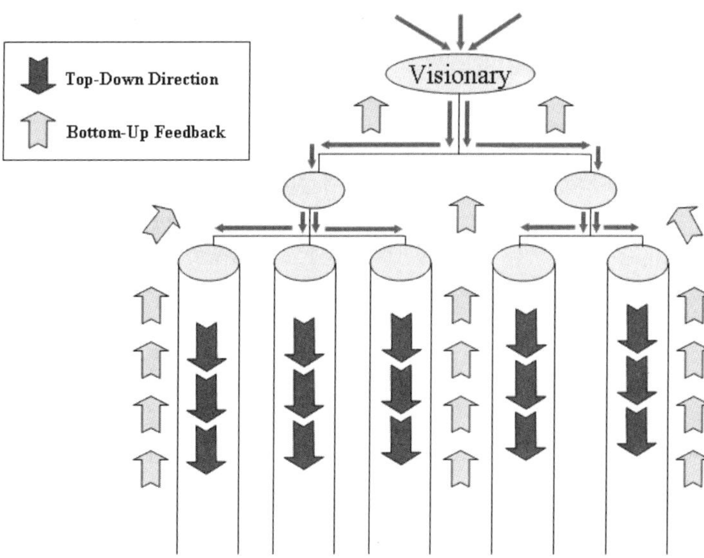


Figure 4. Organization Aligned under a Common Vision

As a declaration of your organization's aspirations, a vision statement should be designed to last forever. It isn't a lofty goal that can be achieved in time, but rather a clear intention that will allow your organization to continuously grow and mature with an unambiguous identity.

A NASA vision statement that simply stated "Putting a Man on the Moon" sounded compelling in the early 1960s, but it didn't carry much weight after Neil Armstrong and his team finally made it to the moon. Here is NASA's current vision statement:

*To improve life here,*
*To extend life to there,*
*To find life beyond*
*...as only NASA can.*

This vision statement has all the ingredients of an effective vision statement—clarity, simplicity, focus, intention, and longevity.

Here are the basic questions you need to answer when you're crafting a vision statement:

- Does it align our capabilities with our potential markets; in other words, is it a clear *effect* of what we do?
- Will it inspire our organization to continuously set and achieve new goals?
- Does it imply excellence in what we do?
- Is it focused enough to keep us from trying to be all things to all people?
- Is it clear and simple enough so that employees at

all levels will be able to articulate and act on it?

## The Mission Statement

Once you've finalized your vision statement, it's time to confirm it. In a mission statement, you identify the *cause* of the effect in the cause-and-effect, or mission-vision, relationship. A mission statement is a clear sentence or short paragraph that establishes your organization's identity by setting the boundaries of what it is and does. By reading between the lines, it should also be obvious what your organization is *not* and what it does *not* do.

A mission statement helps organizations of all shapes and sizes to stay on track and continue to do what they are good at and what they are meant to do. Your mission statement should not, however, be so limiting or time relevant that it keeps your organization from continuously evolving and developing your people, products, and markets.

Microsoft's focused mission statement suggests limitless possibility:

> *At Microsoft, we work to help people and businesses throughout the world realize their full potential.*

Let's examine just what makes this an effective mission statement. First, it clearly outlines what Microsoft does now and will do in the future, which is to help people and businesses throughout the world reach their full potential. Second, it doesn't limit Microsoft to the software or computer products we associate with them today.

For all we know, based on its innovation over the past two decades, Microsoft could be developing new tools that will work in a completely new medium. As long as it's working towards the realization of people's and businesses' full potential, it's still in alignment with its mission.

Adding the phrase "through innovative computer software" to the end of its mission statement would limit the thoughts and actions of individual workers at Microsoft. Employees striving to create new breakthroughs in technology would be limited to software-based innovation. While they're focusing on that, a company with a broader mission might be focusing on the next generation to emerge after software. In time, this could render Microsoft's products, as well as its research and development pipeline, obsolete.

When crafting your organization's mission statement, ask yourself the following questions:

- Does it provide appropriate boundaries for what we are, or will be capable of achieving?
- Does it effectively describe the *cause* from which the vision statement will be realized?
- Does it allow sufficient room for flexibility and growth of core competencies?
- Does it imply excellence in what we do?
- Is it focused enough to keep us from trying to be all things to all people?
- Is it unambiguous and simple enough so that employees at all levels will be able to articulate it and act within its boundaries?

As you can see, there are some similarities in the criteria for developing vision and mission statements. But while a vision statement tends to be goal-oriented, a mission statement focuses more on an organization's boundaries. Because of the similarities, some companies have successfully merged their vision and mission statements into one. This is fine, as long as the criteria for both are incorporated into a single statement that doesn't violate the rule of simplicity.

Let's take a look at one example of an effective combined vision and mission statement. Brown-Forman is the parent company of Jack Daniels, Southern Comfort, and many other well-known spirit and wine labels. It also makes many consumer durables products, including Lenox and Dansk china, crystal, and dishware. How can spirits and dishware come together in one vision? Without a clear vision/mission statement, it would be easy to jump to the conclusion that this is a highly confused company with little or no sense of who they are. But their vision/mission statement makes it all clear:

*Be the best brand builder in the industry, period!*

As we can now see, Brown-Forman is focused primarily on building product brands. Assuming that they have already bought, or will buy, a quality product with market potential, their growth depends on their ability to brand it in the marketplace. Simply stated, their mission is to make their products more recognizable by consumers through effective marketing and advertising capabilities.

If Brown-Forman's vision/mission statement were to "be the number one distributor of liquor and wine," it would have trouble working with the china and crystal companies it has acquired, because its core competencies would be focused on spirits. A simple, but clear shift in wording can make a world of difference in how your organization allots its capital and other resources to achieve success.

## Core Values

A vision statement will steer you in the desired direction for growth and development, while the mission statement will keep you from expanding in an unfocused, uncontrolled manner. These statements are like filters that allow you to develop new strategies while keeping you in a focused, yet flexible, pattern of development. The third filter is your organization's core values.

In a new organization, the founders typically establish core values in order to guide the behaviors and decisions of all employees and alliance partners. If for some reason an existing organization hasn't established its core values, its leadership team, in conjunction with its stakeholders and employees, can do so by using available techniques that will help them draw out desirable ones.

The intention is to develop a culture that's in line with those values and in which each stakeholder makes decisions that are in alignment with them. In order for this to be successful, an organization must develop its core values with clear reasoning and conviction, ensure that they are communicated clearly to each employee, and periodically reinforce them.

The Sonoma Valley Museum of Art (SVMA) is a highly successful nonprofit art museum located in Northern California. While helping them develop a new strategic plan, I realized that they didn't have a clear set of core values to use as a filter while determining their new strategic objectives. Using an Appreciative Inquiry technique, they assembled the staff, the board of directors, and key founders of the museum in one room and began to share their peak experiences—those times each person had felt a true sense of self-actualization and connection—during their tenure at the museum.

The peak experiences of each participant were recorded, and the group was then asked to assign a value that captured the essence of each peak experience. When the group completed its list, it was quite evident which values were the most common. An action team was then formed to take the common values and put them in the context of the museum's desired cultural attributes. These core values now guide SVMA toward the museum's desired behaviors and culture:

## COMMUNITY

SVMA exists to enrich the society of which it is a part and to play a vital role in bringing art to diverse segments, thus inspiring the common and individual interests of the community.

## ENGAGEMENT

SVMA is profoundly involved with the activities and interests of its members, its community, and its visitors. It seeks to be an active center for fellowship, cultural inquiry, and discovery through art.

## INCLUSIVENESS

SVMA connects people through art and is a museum for people of all ages and backgrounds. It is comprehensive in its scope and vision.

## EXCELLENCE

SVMA is committed to quality. Its enduring goal is to provide its community with art, in all its diverse forms and media, at the highest levels of imagination, skill, and talent.

## INTEGRITY

SVMA seeks a position of trust in its community. It is resolved to operate within the most scrupulous bounds of sincerity, good faith, professionalism, and honor.

Core values that are generated from appreciative inquiry methods like this one are useful in identifying viable strategies that align with an organization's values, and weeding out those that are not in alignment. The museum later used these core values as a litmus test to determine whether each strategy they envisioned was worth pursuing, from an emotional perspective. As a result, the strategic plan served as an unanticipated catalyst that ultimately led to the alignment the staff, the board of directors, and even the greater community behind the new direction.

### *Organizational Knowledge*

Knowledge is a basic requirement for any organization. Though it's often confused with information, organizational knowledge makes existing information immediately useful and of value to some person or part of the organization. As figure 5 illustrates, effective organizational knowledge takes appropriate timing, context, and accessibility as well as information.

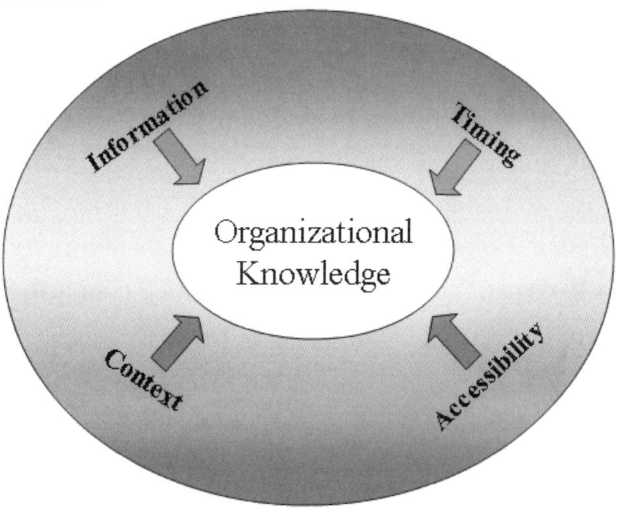


Figure 5. Organizational Knowledge

Knowledge management has been in the forefront of the minds of organizational leaders since the 1980s, yet very few have successfully deployed it in their organizations. Managing knowledge is a challenge both because of the complexity of knowledge itself and because knowledge means different things to different people. If you don't understand what organizational knowledge is, you'll chase after fragments of information that are untimely, inaccessible, and out of context for most people. Without definition, hit or miss is about the best you can do.

You also need to understand the different kinds of knowledge and have a way to access the appropriate type in a timely manner. Here are just some of the knowledge types you'll need to consider when you're developing an organizational knowledge model for your company.

### *Tacit Knowledge*

Tacit knowledge cannot be readily transferred or documented because it's based on personal wisdom or experience and so resides in a person's head. An example of tacit knowledge might be a specific employee's ability to anticipate a key customer's reaction to a planned change based on that employee's experience with that particular customer.

### *Skill-Based Knowledge*

Skill-based knowledge is occupational knowledge that is immediately transferable only to a person with a similar skill set. Skill-based knowledge can often be transferred through documented training exercises or help guides. However, some experience is usually required to complete the knowledge transfer.

### *Process Knowledge*

Process knowledge is the knowledge of an organizational process required to complete a business cycle. This kind of knowledge requires an understanding of specific steps and can usually be transferred by combining process flows and narratives. Depending on the complexity of the process at hand, some experience may be necessary to ensure successful knowledge transfer.

### *Documented Knowledge*

Documented knowledge typically doesn't require any type of experience or walk-through and can be stored and indexed easily in a database. It can range from sample reports to presentations provided by various vendors. The key to successfully managing documented knowledge is indexing it properly so it's available to all relevant inquiry.

### *Performance Knowledge*

Performance knowledge is intended to steer your organization toward the desired results. Based on appropriate metrics, it comes from reports generated at all levels of the organization—personnel productivity, department or divisional performance, management dashboards, strategic scorecards, and the like. Data warehouses, or fully integrated enterprise resource planning systems, are typically used to collect this information and filter it into meaningful reports to managers at all levels.

### *Complex Knowledge*

Complex knowledge can be any combination of the knowledge types described above and may come in the form of a methodology. For example, if a research department of a drug company wants to initiate a drug discovery, it will need documentation on existing compounds, knowledge of development processes, and inputs from scientists who have developed similar drugs in the past. In fact, some of this knowledge may have to be imported from outside the organization from professional networks, contract scientists, publications, and the Internet. Once the process of discovery begins, performance reports can be used to track the success of the initiative.

A well-designed knowledge management system is only as good as the company culture in which it operates. An organization must continuously foster the development of its employees through training and teaching. Training in itself can be very effective in building the know-how and skills of employees, but if your organization can foster a culture dedicated to both learning and teaching, it will have the potential to reach a perpetual state of workforce excellence—a state very few organizations have achieved thus far.

## Organizational Intelligence

Another key requirement for any organization is the ability to acquire, develop, and use intelligence. Organizational intelligence differs from organizational knowledge in that it focuses not just on the organization's internal dynamics, but also on its ability to understand and anticipate the future actions of customers, markets, partners, suppliers, and competitors. Organizational intelligence depends on a combination of strong relationships, resources, effective analytical models, a robust information infrastructure, and, of course, wisdom. Intelligence systems analyze all the organization's interdependencies and relationships and then provide the means of simulating various business scenarios that will allow management to make more informed decisions.

The absolute minimum requirement of organizational intelligence is to integrate the flow of information between your organization's supply side and sell side. Without this, accumulated intelligence will break down and eventually lead to dissipation, misinterpretation, and inaction.

As your own internal integration and information sharing begin to improve, you'll become more capable of gathering, interpreting, and acting on information about your customers and consumers. The more information you have about your customers and the greater your ability to interpret and act upon this information, the better you'll be able to retain them by developing and nurturing relationships that add value.

The ultimate objective is to move from a position of reacting to your customers' demands to anticipating their needs and providing the goods and services that will allow them to go to the next level of performance in their own markets. This type of intelligence allows a company to not only increase its top line through existing products and services, but also to experience exponential growth by creating new products, services, and even sales channels.

Customer relationship and trade promotion management systems are tools that can enable you to track each interaction with the customer, track and manage your sales pipeline, and measure and optimize the effectiveness of your general marketing and trade promotion campaigns. They can also track sales effectiveness and win/loss scenarios that can ultimately lead to improved sales and marketing performance and reduce threats presented by the competition.

Supply-side intelligence is yet another means of achieving highly desirable reduction in cost and improvement in quality. The more information you're able to accumulate about your suppliers' average cycle time, availability of product, perfect order delivery, and so on, the more you'll be able to generate leverage with them through strategic sourcing. Gathering information on the comparative performance of your various suppliers, and presenting this information to them when bargaining for future service and raw material contracts, allows you to negotiate the best possible deal.

Information tools such as supplier relationship management systems allow you to track historical transactions with each vendor and to evaluate their pricing and performance over time based on a standard set of pre-established business rules. These tools can dramatically reduce the time required to collect and decipher information and present compelling reports to your suppliers, thereby putting the power of leverage on your side.

• • •

## Tips for Small Companies and Nonprofits

Crafting vision and mission statements and developing core values is just as important for small companies and nonprofits as it is for larger organizations. Doing this early on in your organization's lifecycle will help you handle all the changes that come with rapid growth and expansion. Adhering to the vision and mission during such times will keep you from losing focus and becoming diluted, which can lead to misallocation of resources and cost overruns.

For smaller organizations to achieve focused growth, developing core values is just as important as the vision and mission statements. The example of core values given in this chapter was, in fact, taken from a smaller, yet highly successful nonprofit museum.

In the early stages of a small organization's lifespan, knowledge management will to a great extent depend on each individual worker. As a leader of such an organization, you should look for opportunities to create repositories for documents that can be reused or recycled, such as proposals, contracts, and product documentation.

• • •

The competitive focus of the first ring of Musashi's book is merely part of the foundation-setting process of rings one through four, which describe all the things you need to prepare you to enter the "enlightened state" of the fifth ring. In this enlightened state the focus shifts towards the reinvention of self through a combination of collective visioning, intention setting, and alignment—all taking place within a continuous creative renewal process. In chaos and complexity theory, this state is called "being on the edge," a phrase mainstream Western society has recently adopted.

Unfortunately, most organizations today lack the culture, tools, and techniques they need to achieve this state. If they do achieve it, it's either through sheer coincidence or some unanticipated disruption in the business environment. In the latter case, it is rarely sustained due to market fluctuations or cultural, seasonal, legislative, and other influences.

In the Book of Earth, Musashi not only focuses on the values, vision, and knowledge needed to build a successful strategy; he also stresses the importance of understanding your own rhythms and those of your surroundings. No matter what size your organization is, if you take a holistic look at its inner workings, you're likely to find opportunities for improving some of the basic processes and practices it needs to achieve strategic excellence. Putting them in place will give you a better understanding of the inner rhythms and patterns constantly emerging in your organization and therefore better equip you either to take advantage of those that are beneficial to you, or to quickly and proactively change when your rhythm is broken or undesirable patterns begin to surface.

In the next chapter you'll learn how rhythm helps you use a sound infrastructure to your advantage. By using the right tools in the right sequence, you'll be able to demonstrate excellence in self-awareness, timing, and targeting with each opportunity for change.

## Chapter 5

# Water: Becoming Fluid

FLUID STRATEGY REQUIRES APPLYING the right tools at the right time to the right target in order to achieve the right objective. This process begins with setting the right intention.

## The Right Intention

In the Book of Water, Musashi insists that the body should never pull the mind along. If you apply this principle to your organization, it means that top management (the mind) will lead the body (the members of the organization) by developing a common intention and getting everyone working toward the same vision. By the same token, the body stimulates the mind with the feedback that allows it to change and adapt.

In my experience, nothing gets this process started faster than total commitment and excitement at the top levels of the organization. Employees inevitably share the excitement and model the behaviors of their bosses. If members of the management team are on board with the vision, they will carry the intention for change down to the next level through their day-to-day interactions. Those who report to them will catch their enthusiasm and begin to believe that these goals can be accomplished. When continuously reinforced through clear and simple communications, eventually each employee will begin to think and act in ways that align with the goal.

The overarching vision must be kept in the forefront of each individual's mind. The sooner everyone buys into the common vision, the more likely it is to be realized. One of the most effective examples of the power of combined vision and alignment is NASA's first moon mission. While just about everybody else in the world doubted NASA's ability to land a man on the moon in such a short period of time, the members the moon mission thought otherwise. One day while a janitor was changing a light bulb in a closet at one of NASA facilities, a reporter asked him what he was doing. "I'm putting a man on the moon!" he replied. NASA's intention was to put a man on the moon, and when everyone in the organization, including the janitor, aligned with that intention, they achieved it. At that point, the leadership set new intentions to direct the body.

Once a strategy, or strategic intention has been established, your organization must implement a process for bridging the gap between strategy and action. In order to achieve success in any strategic initiative, you must have a means to execute strategy and collect feedback from all levels of the organization. This, in turn, fuels the next strategic cycle.

# The Right Tools

## *Opportunity Analysis*

Over the past few decades, many organizations, from the departmental level all the way up to corporate headquarters, have used a SWOT (strengths, weaknesses, opportunities and threats) analysis because it is easy to use and adds to perceived value. I have created a derivative of the SWOT, which I call the *opportunity analysis*, which tends to be much more useful, and a lot less confusing. The opportunity analysis, like the SWOT, should be used as a foundation-setting tool, and not as a primary strategy development tool.

The traditional SWOT analysis forces us to view *opportunities* as equal, yet separate entities to the strengths, weaknesses and threats. The opportunity analysis differs in that it extracts opportunities from the existing strengths, weaknesses, threats and relationships, allowing each category to be viewed as a set of new possibilities, as opposed to an isolated condition, and it inspires focus on the positive rather than the negative.

At this stage, the purpose of an opportunity analysis is to fill any existing gaps. The opportunity analysis is a very helpful tool in generating organizational self-awareness. It will help you identify organizational and process gaps that can prevent you from executing your new strategies, while considering new opportunities for filling them.

The opportunity chart (figure 6) is the optimal way to display the results of the opportunity analysis.

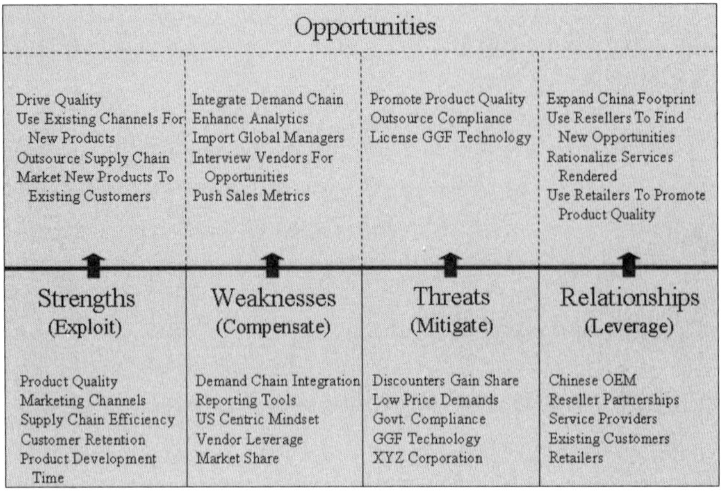


Figure 6. Example of an Opportunity Chart

The information in the chart is derived either by a collaborative group process or by having the leadership team fill out a questionnaire. While I'm a huge fan of collaborative workshops, I also believe that administering the opportunity analysis by means of a questionnaire can save much valuable executive time. The questionnaire is quite simple and normally consists of the following questions:

1. What are the top five strengths of our organization, and how can they be leveraged?
2. What are the five severest weakness of our organization, and how can they be compensated?
3. What are the five severest threats (internal or external) that put our organization at risk, and how can they best be mitigated?

4. What are the top five relationships or strategic alliances that should be leveraged?

The objective of an opportunity analysis is to collect as many of the questionnaires as possible from the management team and to record the results in a central database. The replies represent the management team's view of the organization's health, so when soliciting input, it's important to include managers from all areas of the business. That way, the analysis will give an accurate representation of the business as a whole.

All similar answers are tallied, and those with the most replies are listed in descending order, starting with the most common response. Typically, only the top five to ten replies are recorded and presented back to management in a format similar to the example in figure 6. The results of the opportunity analysis are then kept until the financial analysis is complete. Together, these analyses provide the information needed to plot your organization's position in the strategic lifecycle.

### *Financial Analysis*

You can use the information made available through knowledge management and organizational reporting and intelligence to perform a financial analysis of your organization. As I've already mentioned, financials should never be used to drive strategy. However, good and timely financial information is an effective performance indicator that can help you steer your organization in the desired direction.

Along with the more intuitive representation provided in the opportunity analysis, your organization's KPIs, if established properly, will help you determine the overall health of your organization and identify opportunities for significant improvement. Your company should take full advantage of its ability to influence these key performance indicators in every way possible.

When assessing the financial performance of a for-profit organization, shareholder value is usually the primary driver. Although many areas outside of the company's sphere of influence (such as market sector performance) affect shareholder value, there are other areas over which a company does have control. In figure 7, the right side shows the KPIs that your company can directly influence. The darker the examples on the left side become, the less likely it is that you can exert influence through direct intervention.

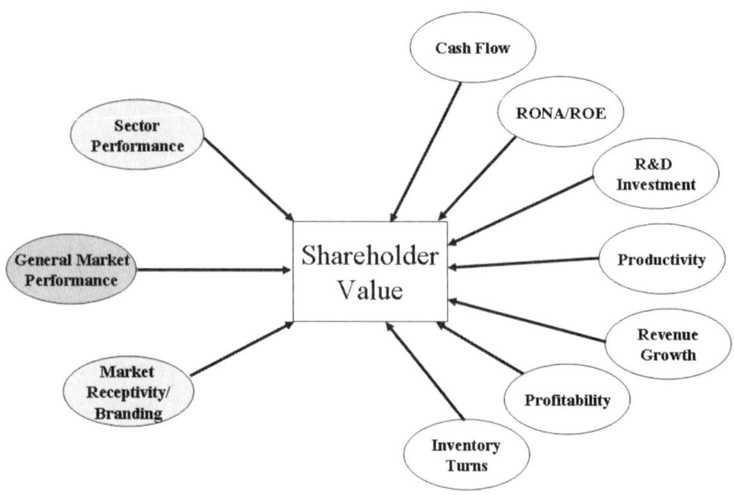


Figure 7. Sources of Shareholder Value

Although a company can influence the sector performance and market receptivity/branding indicators, it normally takes a creative organizational leap to do so. Plugging the organizational gaps that exist today will prepare you to achieve this in the future.

## Common KPIs

While the following key performance indicators don't include all the financial data that needs to be tracked, they highlight some of the more important areas of intervention.

### *Cash Flow*

Cash flow represents the financial health of an organization. You should track cash flow trends over the past one to three years and analyze them to determine whether or not you'll have sufficient cash on hand to meet current and future plans for expansion. You should also review your long-term and total debt and compare it to industry averages. Be aware of when cash decreases over time, while debt simultaneously continues to rise.

### *RONA/ROE*

These indicators help you determine the overall effectiveness of your company's management. Return on net assets (RONA) helps to determine the return that management has achieved based on available assets. Return on equity (ROE) shows how much management has earned on the capital made available through shareholders.

### *R & D Investment*

R & D investment can either be too high or too low, depending on your industry and the success rate of your previous pipeline products. You should analyze and compare your overall investment with peer companies. You will need to communicate with shareholders to justify any over- or underinvestment. On the other hand, as you become more of a visionary company, you'll tend to pay less attention to this KPI. However, you'll need to justify any deviations from the norm in your annual report.

### *Productivity*

Productivity, or gross margin per employee, is based on the amount of revenue, or profit, that comes into your company per employee. The more revenue per employee, the more productive your company is overall.

### *Revenue Growth*

To determine overall growth or decline, you should track revenue growth, or top-line performance, by product or service over a one-to-three year period of time, as well as quarter-to-quarter trends and seasonality. Revenue growth evaluated in conjunction with profitability indicates the sustainability of a particular product or service.

### *Profitability*

You should track both net profit margin and operating margin over time and analyze and compare them with peer companies in your industry. Even with highly efficient processes, decreased profits over time may indicate that external competitive threats are driving down the price of your product or service or taking over your market share, which would indicate a need for innovative change.

### *Inventory Turns*

Inventory turns indicate how quickly you are recouping capital tied up in inventory. In addition to indicating high or low efficiency in turnover, decreasing turns can indicate slow sales, while increasing turns normally indicate sales growth.

### *Sector Performance*

Sector performance is an indicator of all companies or divisions in a particular market sector, such as life sciences, consumer products, or retail. While stimulating sector performance is difficult, you can do it through creative marketing.

### *Market Receptivity and Branding*

Influencing market receptivity to a new or improved product, as well as branding it effectively, is also difficult. To do this, you need to devise strong strategies to create demand. This requires a fully integrated organization that allows all areas to influence the product over its development lifecycle.

### *General Market Performance*

General market performance is the most difficult indicator to influence. As we've witnessed in recent recessions caused by the bursting dot-com bubble and the 9/11 terrorist attacks, there's not much one company can do to rejuvenate a sagging global market. However, introducing innovative ideas can neutralize the threat of a down market.

The data pertaining to each of these indicators should be collected and recorded over time using a financial tool that allows for graphical representation of data. This new information should then be given to the leadership team so it can evaluate, discuss, and question the relevancy of each indicator. After the leadership team members review and discuss this information, they should evaluate it in light of the opportunity analysis to identify both favorable and unfavorable trends. When they've done this, they're ready to plot the company's position in the strategic lifecycle.

## The Right Time

Strategic lifecycle plotting allows you to develop a true awareness of who you are as an organization at any given time by showing you where you stand from the perspective of your company's entire lifecycle. Smaller companies that have one product, or a grouping of similar products, can use the lifecycle plotting technique for their entire company. Larger companies will want to plot individual product or service divisions, evaluating them first individually and then collectively as a portfolio.

The lifecycle plotting process begins with leadership team members reviewing and discussing the results of the strategic opportunity and financial analyses. Once they have a firm understanding of their company's key performance indicators and opportunities, the plotting can begin. Plotting discussions begin within one of the given quadrants of the lifecycle chart (figure 8).

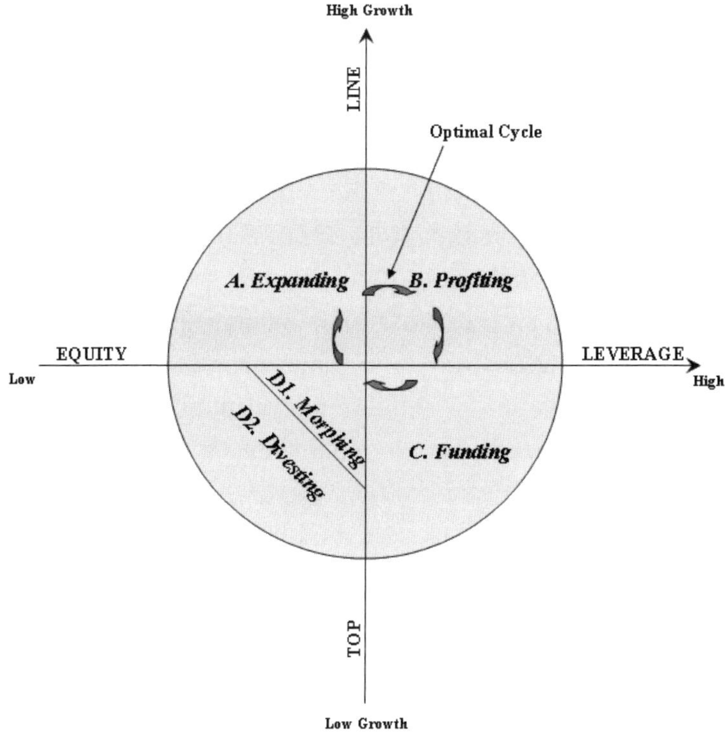


Figure 8. Strategic Lifecycle Chart

The lifecycle chart is a qualitative tool that requires ample justification through quantitative financial analysis. The chart is divided into four quadrants, each formed by two axes of significance: top-line growth (vertical) and equity leverage (horizontal). The top-line axis represents the rate at which the top line, or sales, is increasing and thus the rate at which your organization is expanding. The equity-leverage axis represents the overall leverage achieved on existing assets. Determining the bottom line is a more complex process, as it takes into account profitability, productivity, and overall efficiency. Return on equity (ROE) is a good key indicator of this, but you should take a more holistic view when plotting along this axis.

A company or product line that's just starting out will normally begin somewhere between the D and A quadrants and then work its way up to the A quadrant as the product begins to catch on in the marketplace and the rate of growth continues. As the entity continues to grow, you should begin to invest in ways that make it more profitable. As it does, it will migrate into the B quadrant. After a product has been on the market for some time, competitive pricing and product obsolescence begin to slow down top-line growth, and the entity moves into the C quadrant.

When your company is in the C quadrant, you'll normally use the profits taken from the depleting product and invest them in designing a new product or in improving the existing one. Otherwise, profit erosion will continue until it forces you into liquidation. As you can see in figure 8, your organization should remain for as long as possible in quadrant B, the most desirable position on the lifecycle.

In figure 9 we see the same lifecycle chart, but this time with the recommended strategic direction of action and priority based on your organization's position within the lifecycle. For example, if your company plots itself between the D and A quadrants, and the top-line growth is trending upward, you're likely to consider a growth strategy consisting of branding and acquisition. If, on the other hand, the growth is trending downward, you may be in serious trouble, as the markets will not react favorably, and you could end up losing capital because of the failure to generate leverage.

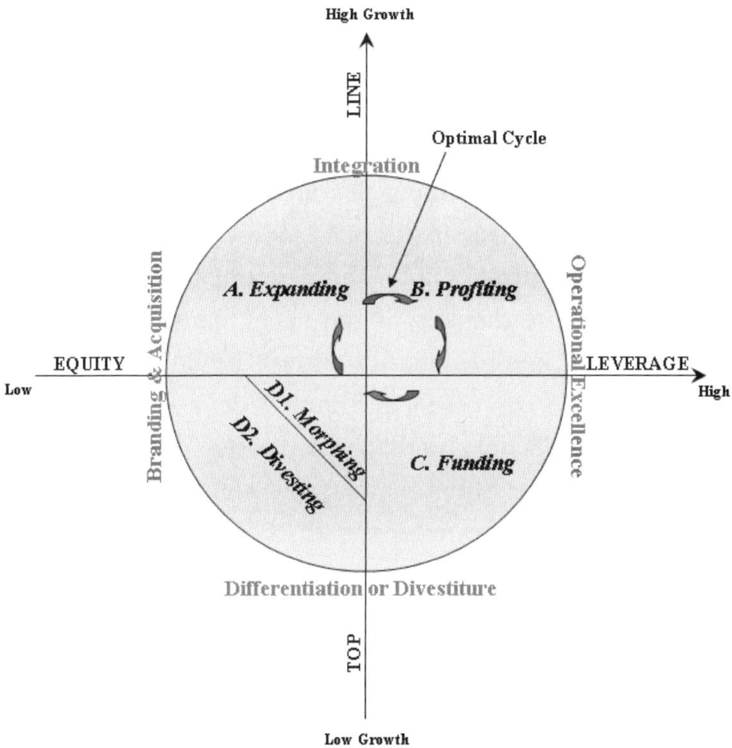


Figure 9. Lifecycle Chart with Strategic Considerations

When your company makes it well into the A quadrant with upward momentum, you should take a close look at its internal infrastructure in search of ways to improve its profitability by integrating its processes. As it starts to move into the B quadrant, you should begin to optimize its organization, processes, and information systems to maximize leverage through operational excellence.

If your company is entering the C quadrant, you should immediately begin looking into either morphing its existing product or creating an entirely new product to replace it, thus rendering obsolete any copycat products on the market. This should be done while you're still in a position of leverage, so the existing product can fund the development of the new or improved replacement. If a product is entering the end of its lifecycle and becoming obsolete, you should divest it while it still has market appeal.

Remaining proactive as the product transitions from one quadrant to the next is the key. Choosing a strategic direction too late essentially allows the body to lead the mind, and this can result in financial devastation. Striking while the iron is hot should be your motto, and you should take proactive steps to remain aware, allowing a financially fruitful transition from one quadrant of the lifecycle to the next.

## The Right Target

Miyamoto Musashi's maxim, "Never let the body pull the mind along," applies not only to timing, but also to strategic targeting. Strategic targeting is based on the portfolio of strategic actions that result from the opportunity analysis, the assessment of key performance indicators during the financial analysis, and the position of your company (or its business units) in the strategic lifecycle.

Strategic lifecycle plotting significantly reduces a company's potential areas of investment. If, for example, your company or business unit plots itself between quadrants B and C, you definitely shouldn't allocate all of your resources to branding initiatives. While some branding may occur at this stage (for example, if market saturation hasn't yet occurred), it shouldn't be a major target for strategic investment. This is more likely a time to start a new visioning cycle to generate new innovative ideas.

Let's say that a company or business unit that plots itself between quadrants B and C has just realized that it's still trending upward with regard to top-line growth. It has also determined via its opportunity analysis that its severest weakness is poor visibility due to inadequate management reporting and analytical capabilities. Additionally, its financial analysis shows that it has a weak position regarding return on equity (ROE) and that its profit margins are less than desirable. Conversations with the chief information officer also reveal that the company is spending more money than its peer companies or competitors in an effort to keep its disparate information systems talking to one another.

If this looks like your company, you now have a clear opportunity to integrate your process, organizational, and information systems. If you wait until your sales growth begins to decline, you may find yourself in the precarious situation of not being able to fund such a large strategic undertaking. You need to invest in integration while shareholder value and growth are still high. Proactive transitions between each quadrant can keep it high and thus avoid extreme fluctuations as a result of untimely decisions. Not allowing the body to pull the mind along will keep your company's strategic development in sync with its markets.

## The New Bottom Line

The term "bottom line" used to pertain only to the financial wellbeing, or profitability of a company. Consumers and shareholders today are becoming much more aware of the world that they live in, and are demanding that companies adopt policies to ensure environmental and social sustainability, in addition to financial health. As the world wakes up to the reality that we can no longer conduct business in the exploitative ways that we have over the past hundred years, businesses will need to change rapidly – not only to adapt to consumer demand, but also to do their part in saving our planet. As a result, some conscientious businesses are beginning to adopt new policies and processes that contribute to a more sustainable way of doing business.

Environmental awareness and sustainability practices, the second bottom line, support the management of risk resulting from corporate processes and practices that could have damaging results on the environment, as well as the company's image and stock performance. As you recall the Exxon Valdez disaster, you will probably also recall the devastating impact it had on Exxon's financial performance over the following years. Today, the world's consumers and shareholders are much more savvy, demanding a higher level of integrity and awareness. Watchdog agencies are rapidly emerging, proactively reporting those companies that do not maintain safe and environmentally sound practices to the public.

Social responsibility is the third bottom line, and focuses on the management of societal risks stemming from incidents that would lead to a damaging affect on local economies and society as a whole. Consider the negative press that certain large "big box" retailers received after small towns began to realize that their entire small business infrastructure, or town center, began to erode. The "big box" stores eventually took away the small shop owners' business, as well as their employees, luring them in with great benefits and higher pay – both of which were skillfully rescinded by these stores, by switching many of their employees to part-time status. Studies began to report on how crime rates were rising in those towns that had a "big box" store in them, and their images began to implode. Certain notorious "big box" stores also began to lose a significant share of their markets to companies like Target and Costco, who were purchasing large quantities of goods from local vendors in the communities in which they operate. Needless to say, the management of social risk can have an ever-increasing impact on a company's image and financial wellbeing.

This *triple bottom line* approach to bottom line analysis will provide your organization with a more holistic and realistic view of risk, image and financial health, allowing it to change non-sustainable practices before you read about them in the newspaper. It is also the prudent thing to do given the recent developments in global climate change – not to mention the rapid industrialization of the developing world, whose countries need to be set on a path of sustainability before it is too late. For those not buying the ethical reasoning, there is also a financial incentive. New financial indexes such as the Dow Jones Sustainability Index, formed in 1999, are now outperforming their more traditional counterparts like the Dow Jones Industrial Index. Regardless of your personal reasons for getting on board with this holistic win-win-win bottom line approach, chances are, most of your employees will be delighted being a part of such a move in the right direction.

• • •

## Tips for Small Companies and Nonprofits

An opportunity analysis is an effective way for small companies and nonprofits to assess the environments in which they operate as they seek opportunities to continuously improve the organization. The opportunity is easy to develop and is best done in smaller organizations with the collaboration of all employees.

Financial analysis is just as important for smaller organizations as it is for larger firms. While maintaining proper books is essential for all companies, many don't begin to use metrics and management-reporting procedures until things begin to go wrong. This is perhaps one of the top reasons that so many small businesses don't make it. Such reporting procedures serve as early warning signs that something may be amiss. Developing them proactively enables you to monitor and manage cash flow and other important metrics. An abundant cash flow can allow you to react rapidly to take advantage of emerging opportunities, while lack of cash flow can lead to unfortunate opportunity loss.

Small organizations should pay close attention to the

strategic lifecycle model. A small company in an expansion mode will usually start out at the bottom of the upper right-hand quadrant. You should monitor your positions in the lifecycle and adopt the recommended strategies, as they will enable you to transition successfully to the next quadrant. If you notice your company going backward in the normal lifestyle pattern of growth, you should review and assess your products or services and your penetration of your marketplace.

• • •

If you adhere to outdated command-and-control structures that rely on five-year plans, your company will be like a rigid oak. It may look stable, but it can topple in a storm. On the other hand, if you apply the principles found in Musashi's Book of Water, you can make your organization like a flexible willow that can not only withstand, but thrive amidst the changing winds of the modern business environment.

In the next chapter we'll examine how your company's various entities need to operate to allow you to continuously manage highly successful strategic initiatives.

# Chapter 6

# Fire: Creative Change

THE FIRE METAPHOR IS about creativity and change. As Musashi explains in the third Ring, Fire implies the point at which the strategy is created and applied. Since the Fifth Ring (see chapter 8) is where the strategies are actually created, this chapter will focus on the importance of allowing momentum and change to occur at the point of execution.

Companies that are continuously successful in their markets aren't afraid of change. In fact, they change quite often and with great momentum. Their ability to react to market dynamics and internal decisions is ingrained both in their infrastructure and their corporate culture. While Part 3 is dedicated to the development and application of new visionary strategies, this chapter explains the structure and processes you'll need to put in place to enable your company to embrace change and begin to execute an increasing number of bold new strategies.

Strategy execution can be quite difficult in larger organizations because of the complexity caused by competing strategic initiatives being carried out simultaneously. Therefore, this chapter will focus mainly on the strategic project and program infrastructure requirements of larger and more complex organizations.

## Program Management Infrastructure

The program management infrastructure is really quite simple. It requires very few full-time resources, if any. It can also consist of a virtual team made up of project managers from each strategic project. However, in this case, one team coordinator should be assigned to oversee the group. The program office is designed to allow strategies to continuously permeate your organization and result in action. New strategies are developed and launched by a senior leadership team, which typically consists of a group of senior managers representing the line functions (such as business units and product divisions) and organizational support functions (such as finance, human resources and information services) that work collaboratively for the good of the company.

Once strategic goals and their supporting initiatives are formalized, they are incorporated into the program management infrastructure for implementation. The program office then coordinates all the ongoing strategic initiatives being implemented simultaneously.

A steering committee is formed, consisting of members of the leadership team who have been identified as stakeholders in the strategies being implemented. Stakeholders are those directly impacted by the strategies. They are the ultimate owners and decision makers of the initiatives at hand.

For example, if a strategy calls for the growth and aggressive market expansion of Product X, steering committee members will likely consist of at least these stakeholders:

- VP of marketing
- VP of sales
- Head of the business unit or product division
- VP of human resources
- Chief information officer
- Chief financial officer

A strategy calling for the improvement or divestiture of a product at the end of its lifecycle might consist of the same members but also include the VP of research and development and the VP of operations. Depending on the strategic significance of the initiative, the CEO may also be involved in the steering committee.

The task of the stakeholders in the steering committee is to ensure the vertical alignment of strategic requirements by passing them down to the program office, which determines the best time and approach for implementing them. Figure 10 shows the desirable alignment of the steering committee, the program office, and the project teams that will implement the strategies.

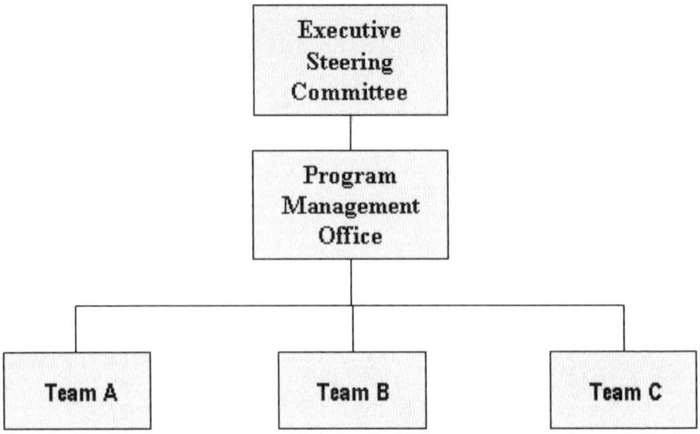


Figure 10. Program Management Infrastructure

You need to be careful not to involve the steering committee in the details of the change activities. The steering committee's job is to sustain the vision created by the leadership team, to ensure that it is effectively communicated to the next levels, and to hold the program and project teams accountable for proper execution of the strategic initiatives at the optimal time.

After the executive steering committee meets with the program management office to discuss the new strategy and determine its priority in the portfolio of current and planned projects, a cross-functional team is assembled to implement the change. The team might consist of people from various departments with various applicable skill sets, but its leader should always be from the business unit impacted.

Too many organizations put support personnel in the lead role to implement strategic projects. For example, they might put a project manager from information services in charge because of his or her expertise in project management. I see this done over and over again, but it's always a mistake, for it eventually leads to applying an information services solution to a business problem.

Projects established to resolve business issues or carry out business strategies should always be led by a person who has the authority and know-how to plan and implement a change that meets the needs of the business and is designed to last. Support personnel and third-party resources can be brought in at any time to provide the team with the specific knowledge needed to successfully execute the change.

Once the strategic requirements have been communicated down to the program office and the implementation teams and the projects are up and running, communicating back up to the senior leadership team through the program office and the steering committee should take place on a regular basis. This continuous down-up-down flow of communication within an approved and mandated structure is vital to the success of any strategic initiative.

Project team leaders need to set up weekly status meetings with the program manager to discuss accomplishments, plans, budgets, and any potential deviations that might add time or cost to the project. The program manager then generates a comprehensive report reflecting the status of each project and communicates this information to the steering committee on a biweekly or monthly basis.

Issues that cannot be resolved within the teams or in conjunction with the program manager are sent up the ladder to the steering committee for resolution. Any issue that can cause an increase in time or budget is immediately moved up to the steering committee for resolution, as are service issues that haven't been resolved within a predetermined period of time.

## The Program Management Office

The program management office (PMO) is where strategy is turned into successful action—in the right way, at the right time. It provides you with the means to manage multiple simultaneous initiatives in a way that creates synergies across them while eliminating redundancy among the various project teams. The program office doesn't usually demand a lot of resources. Typically, it consists of a full-time program manager responsible for the coordination of all strategic projects. Some program offices will include a change-management expert and an administrative assistant to help with the large volume of documentation and templates and the coordination effort that takes place on a daily basis.

Many organizations choose not to establish a program office. Some don't think it's necessary because they don't have a lot of strategic changes taking place. This is usually because the organization resists change and is waiting for the marketplace to tell it what to do next. Other companies don't have a program office because teams work on projects individually, disconnected from the rest of the organization and other strategic action teams. This is a sign of fragmentation. In such cases, project teams working simultaneously and using different tools and standards compete for the same resources and often develop redundant solutions for the business.

All companies can benefit from the program management office model depicted in figure 11. It's a useful and highly effective model consisting of eight elements, each of which works to ensure that value is being delivered at each stage of every project and across all projects.

Figure 11. The Program Management Office Model

## *Leadership*

The primary role of the program management office is to provide leadership to all people and entities involved in strategic initiatives. As new project teams are assembled, the PMO works with the individual project managers and team leaders to make sure they can manage a milestone-driven initiative that might have interdependencies with other such initiatives. While this may sound very simple, one of the biggest challenges of running a project in an operationally minded company is managing the milestones to ensure that the project remains on time and on budget.

Team members usually don't have experience managing situations in which each new task presents new challenges on a daily basis. That's because they have been pulled from their operational jobs, in which they are accustomed to performing routine work, whether it be in daily, weekly, or monthly cycles. They need advice, tools, standards, and oversight to make them successful in their new role.

Program managers should hold an orientation for new project team members and supplement it with the on-boarding packages and training relevant to their specific role. Throughout the duration of any project, they need to monitor the activities of each team through periodic meetings and provide guidance when it's needed. As they monitor each project, they can identify and act upon opportunities for cross-project leverage. Once the strategy has been communicated down from the leadership team, the success or failure of any supporting initiative begins with the ability of the PMO to prepare and develop each project team through effective leadership.

### *Knowledge Management*

Knowledge management plays a specific role in the program management office. The PMO provides each project team with a means of tracking plans, progress, issues, risks, and overall requirements. This information is tracked in a standardized way in each team so that it can be easily read and understood by anyone who needs to review it when moving from one team to another. The following list provides a small sample of the hundreds, and even thousands, of knowledge sources tracked and managed by the PMO across all projects:

- Strategic objectives and guidelines
- Project plans
- Project definitions
- Project requirements
- Project tools and methodologies
- Documentation standards and templates
- Communication schedules
- Subject matter expertise
- Meeting schedules
- Project metrics and scorecards
- Sample project deliverables

In order for the knowledge management component of the PMO to be successful, all team members must know that the PMO is their primary source of information for items not available to them within their respective teams. Furthermore, the PMO serves as a conduit to the entire organization with regard to the anticipated change and the progress of the project.

### *Stakeholder Management*

Strategy stakeholders often aren't accustomed to providing guidance to the teams responsible for implementing a strategy. They depend on the program office to tell them how, when, and to what extent they should interact with the teams. They need to be told when it's time for them to make decisions and when to allow the teams themselves to make decisions. The program office maintains a plan that dictates points of interaction and moves any issues that demand immediate resolution up the ladder to stakeholders.

### *Administration*

Although simplicity and standardization are the keys to reducing overhead and mismanagement in the PMO, in large organizations the administrative responsibilities of the program office can be overwhelming. Administering standard tools and templates, evaluating and comparing budgets, and providing reports to project teams and senior management are just a few of its many responsibilities.

Larger organizations usually assign at least a part-time administrative assistant to the project office to lessen the number of tedious administrative tasks that can take the program manager away from value-added activities. In large centralized corporate environments, it may be necessary to have several program offices at the business unit level, all of which report to a centralized corporate PMO.

### *Change Management*

Proper change management is one of the most crucial factors in implementing a successful strategic initiative. But because of its complexity and the depth and breadth of skills required to execute it, many companies either ignore change management or consider it just an occasional team-building exercise. Successful change management usually requires a dedicated or part-time expert in the program office who focuses on, at minimum, the following initiatives:

- Assessing the organization's readiness for change
- Developing a customized change management strategy
- Developing a communication strategy and detailed plan
- Assessing the impacts of proposed changes in each business area
- Managing deviations from planned change (i.e., change control)
- Coaching stakeholders on how to craft their communications
- Coordinating frequent company and departmental change discussions
- Providing direction and guidance to the training team
- Continuously fostering organization-wide buy-in for the change

In addition to meeting these basic requirements, change management experts continuously monitor the organization to detect any source of fear or resistance to change. When they find it, they immediately develop an effective intervention.

### *Resource Management*

The program manager must ensure that the right resources are assigned to each project and then monitor the progress of each team. Allocating resources properly often requires pre-selection interviews and qualification reviews. Since some participants continue to hold operational responsibilities while working on their extra-operational team assignments, the program manager needs to lobby management to ensure that all receive fair and equitable incentives that will guide them toward desirable team behavior and milestone success.

The program manager will also ensure that proper recognition is given to those who fulfill their duties as planned, and especially to those who go above and beyond their prescribed duties to help others meet their targets. On the other hand, the program manager must also make the call when project managers or project team members aren't making the grade.

In larger corporate environments, several project teams are usually implementing strategic initiatives simultaneously. Since many of these initiatives will eventually require integration, certain experts will need to work on more than one project. To make certain that their team receives adequate access to these experts, individual project managers have a tendency to compete for their time. In such cases, the program manager, much like a referee, will need to intervene and devise a schedule that distributes the experts' time fairly among various projects.

### *Scope Management*

If left to itself, project scope tends to take on a life of its own. As soon as employees begin to see the new opportunities for improvement their project provides, they start increasing its scope. While this is a sign that they are truly interested in obtaining the best for their department, one simple rule of economics must be recognized: *Scope increase impacts time, resources and budget*

Whenever the scope of any project begins to creep beyond what was originally planned and several projects running simultaneously begin to push for precious time, limited resources and budget, the program manager must institutionalize a change control process. This process will require that proposed scope changes be supported by a viable business case that clearly demonstrates its value given the effort it will take to implement it.

If the business case justifies enlarging the scope of a project, the program manager must determine if there are sufficient funds to cover the change, or if other scope items of lesser value will need to be put on hold in order to pay for the more valuable change. While scope creep can seldom be completely avoided, you can minimize it through proper planning and team education before the project begins.

This type of portfolio management, when coupled with extensive pre-project planning, brings high value to the organization and can prevent projects from recklessly spending beyond their allocated thresholds.

### *Risk Management*

Program risk management monitors and manages all relevant risks using a central repository and management tool. The objective of centralized risk management is to ensure the highest quality, while minimizing the potential damage that can occur as a result of risk in a particular area. Risk management begins well before a project is kicked off and includes, at a minimum, monitoring the following areas:

- Strategic alignment
- Project planning and scope
- Project interdependencies
- Resistance to change
- Technology obsolescence
- Third-party supplier viability
- Technology development and infrastructure
- Key resource involvement
- Project complexity and size
- Budgetary issues
- Project-related documentation requirements
- Task execution
- Performance and acceptance testing
- Pre- and post-implementation training

This list consists of just those risk areas that are most commonly seen in a program environment. While it's a good place to begin, the list will certainly grow as the program office gains experience.

## Breaking the Operational Chain

The only key milestone individuals in most organizations ever achieve is the one they meet at the end of their daily, weekly, or monthly routine operational cycles. In my career as a strategic advisor, I've been inside of thousands of organizations of all sizes in all industries, and I have found that this is the most common challenge to initiating strategic change without deploying a large external consulting force.

Strategic change cannot happen solely by hiring a consulting team to come in and do it all for you. It requires key individuals from within the organization working in teams to build new capabilities. When putting together strategic project teams, you'll want to engage the best and brightest individuals in your organization. But you can't just throw inexperienced employees into a strategic project team, develop a plan with unidentified milestones, and then expect them to successfully manage these milestones to completion on time and on budget. Strategic change means creating a culture of change.

This isn't as difficult as you might expect, but it takes some dedication and effort. There are many ways to introduce the workforce to ongoing extra-operational activities. However, it all begins with a shared attitude of continuous improvement in each division, department, or even office. Organizations that have employees experienced in working on extra-operational initiatives have a distinct advantage over those who don't. Such employees have experienced achievements that go beyond their day-to-day work, and they've learned to balance routine operational tasks with work on new developments.

Adopting an attitude of continuous improvement starts at the top. Instituting a culture of change can range from requiring vast changes, like those imposed on General Electric by former CEO Jack Welch, to merely requesting small new strategic developments within each division or department on a regular basis until change becomes the norm.

Although the Fifth Ring Strategy process is perhaps the most effective means of driving continuous strategic change and improvement, periodically upping the ante on performance metrics will also drive short-term positive change if done with care. On the other hand, this technique has been drastically abused in recent years, and must be done with care to avoid burning out your employees. Besides increasing shareholder value, if executed thoughtfully, this can temporarily add value to different parts of the organization, either by unleashing creativity with each new solution introduced, or by exposing pockets of incompetence that require additional support and development. Once an organization adopts change as the norm, it will be ready and able to handle more frequent changes that have greater impact.

• • •

## Tips for Small Companies and Nonprofits

Program management for smaller companies and nonprofits isn't normally necessary, as their small size and head count make them highly flexible and adaptable. Such organizations rely more on informal communication and collaboration. Affiliated individuals and volunteers are often a common source of ideas and labor.

That said, even smaller organizations need to be able to apply new strategies in a timely manner when old ideas become obsolete or ineffective. Maintaining a strategic focus will allow you to adapt more effectively when market environments change. Too often, smaller companies and nonprofits are founded on a niche idea, which can last only so long. Nothing remains unique for long, especially if it has a high degree of value to add. Before you know it, you'll find copycats forming all around you!

Nonprofit organizations should engage their board of directors or trustees in developing and executing new strategies. Although board members work on a volunteer basis, they usually have access to other resources and funding sources in the local community, and they're more than willing to help when asked. Planning for succession and recruiting future board members should also be considered in your strategy. You should seek new board members who have the skills and access necessary to achieve your organization's strategic objectives.

• • •

One of the most important things any organization can do is to completely abandon the notion that things can ever remain in a stable state. Although today no astute organizational leaders would admit they're striving for a permanent state of stability, they still tend to wait until shareholder demand, competitive threats, product obsolescence, or antiquated technologies force their organization out of hibernation and into action.

As soon as you embrace the inevitability of change, you can begin to influence it, and thus your organization's creativity and adaptability. By using attractors such as a strong, unified vision, intention, and commitment, you can foster creativity at all levels, leading to breakthroughs that support your vision in ways you never could have imagined.

Vision-based thought in the minds of tens, hundreds,

and sometimes thousands of workers make their jobs more meaningful. And you'll be amazed at how innovative their solutions turn out to be. You'll also have to deal less and less with the turnover of key employees. In the next chapter, you'll see how you can create a culture of continuous strategic change that keeps the best and brightest prospects knocking on your door in search of meaningful employment.

## Chapter 7

# Wind: Knowing How and When to Change

IN THE BOOK OF Wind, Musashi encourages you not to focus on a single technique, but rather to allow all techniques to flow together in one continuous, fluid motion. Timing and rhythm combined play an essential role in the fourth ring. As Musashi explains, speed is of less significance than knowing your opponent's rhythms and how moving in with just the right action at just the right time far exceeds the effectiveness of speed alone.

As you continuously strive to generate new ideas and breakthroughs, you must understand not only your organization's capacity to adopt and support the new ideas, but also the rhythms and timing of your general consumer, your direct customers, and your competitors. This is the knowledge you need to get your organization off the beaten path of incremental development.

In learning how and when to change, the first thing to consider is the fitness landscape, for it will help you understand the importance of continuous reinvention and strategic innovation.

The Fitness Landscape

The fitness landscape uses a metaphor of peaks and valleys to describe the fitness level of an organization. The higher your company sits on the fitness scale—that is, the closer it is to a peak—the more success it's going to experience. Landing on a peak of the fitness landscape through new innovative ideas means higher economic return, less initial competition, and a better chance of creating and leading new markets and channels.

Figure 12 depicts a fitness landscape in which the peaks and valleys represent a higher or lower degree of fitness based on incremental change.

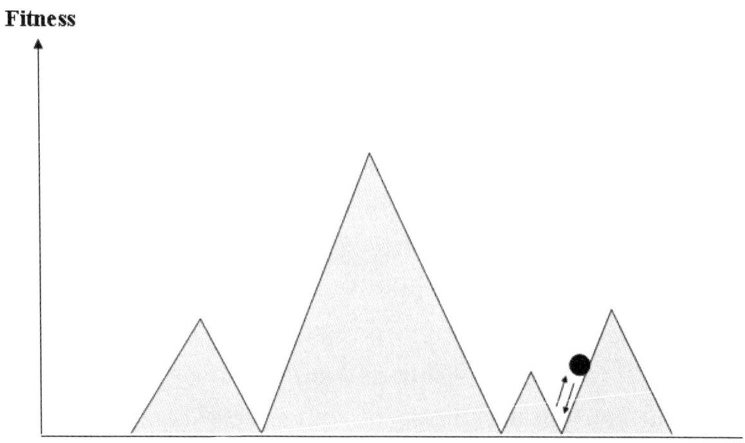


Figure 12. Fitness Landscape with Incremental Change

If the company (the black dot) in figure 12 attempts to reach the peak of the path it's on through incremental change, it will most likely experience a serics of up-and-down movements. As the company makes operational changes to improve its product's performance, it will tend to move upward towards the peak. But because the changes are incremental, they don't produce any radically innovative ideas for the organization, its product, or the development of its markets and channels. As a result, the company will occasionally slide backwards due to one or more of the following external forces:

- Decreased market share gains
- Competitive product improvements
- Competitive promotions and marketing campaigns
- Core technology obsolescence
- Product obsolescence
- Market saturation

Such backsliding forces will make it quite difficult and costly for this company's product to make it to the top of the market. This doesn't mean that a highly competitive product line *can't* make it to the top; it just means that it's less likely to occur through incremental action at the operational level. At best, reaching the peak will be a long road.

The fitness landscape rests on the assumption that changes in an organization's strategy will force all connected systems and processes into a state of upheaval as they try to meet the new demands, thereby moving the organization farther and farther away from a state of stability. When all related systems begin to experience such change, they have more opportunity to reinvent themselves for the better, which in turn keeps them out of the valley and moves them toward the peak.

Buying into radical, non-incremental change through blue-sky visioning will open up new opportunities and exciting possibilities for your organization. Companies that create ongoing change through continuous improvement and radical innovation are more likely to come up with new ideas that will catapult them to the top of a new peak—one that they, or any of their competitors, weren't even aware existed. In figure 13 we see the same company after it initiated a radically new strategic idea.

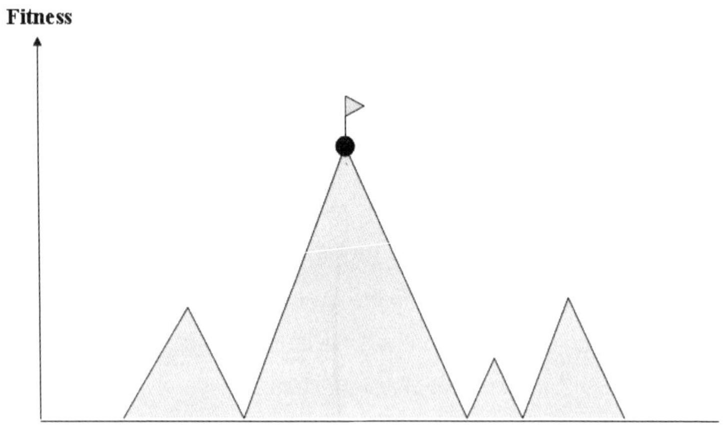


Figure 13. Fitness Landscape with Radical Innovation

A radical new idea is more likely to land you at the top of a new peak because it's more than just an incremental change from a previous state. It starts out at the top of the peak, not in the valley, because there's no competition at this stage. It's brand new, and those who introduce new ideas to the market have many advantages over those who merely follow.

Keep in mind, however, that this company isn't likely to remain at the peak forever. It will need to continuously change its strategy so that it doesn't atrophy or lose its position to a competitor. After the idea is introduced, it will take time for others to copy or follow suit. Therefore, your company must never rest on its laurels. You need to begin immediately to advance new ideas that will take your newborn product or service to the next level while you continue to vision for new ideas.

Although maintaining a continuous flow of radical new ideas and breakthroughs is highly important, without impeccable timing, it can end up hurting you in the long run. You need to make certain that the market is ready for your product. If the idea is too radical, it may be too advanced for the time and force the public to break habits they have developed over the years. Introducing ideas that the public isn't ready for has happened again and again in the past, and it has always ended in economic disaster.

The Ford Edsel comes to mind. It was an automobile with a radical new style, push-button transmission, and a floating speedometer with a built-in warning light. But the public wasn't ready to change the way they interacted with their automobiles. That, coupled with an economic recession, turned the car into a major loss for the Ford Motor Company and was quickly pulled from the marketplace. That and other timing blunders show that being first-to-market doesn't guarantee success.

While landing on a peak with a new idea at the right time can be to your advantage, the idea must also be sustainable. Many software and computer companies in the early to mid-

1980s were unable to hold on to their lead positions because they failed to improve their products in a timely manner. Without a culture that thrives on change, the idea is likely to be passed along to another, more adaptable organization.

## Feedback and the Embedded Alignment Cycle

An organization that possesses the proper infrastructure and is both horizontally and vertically aligned will be able to change much more rapidly, while still balancing the multiple strategic initiatives needed to achieve successful implementation.

In such organizations, information is allowed to flow freely in any direction. As when a rock is thrown into the middle of a pond, concentric rings of information ripple farther and farther out, making it possible to communicate each action to be taken to everyone impacted by that change.

Once the leadership team has aligned itself on a new strategy through the collaborative visioning process described in Chapter 8, its participants pass the strategy along to each level and department in the organization. As each impacted department or team works to implement the change, they generate feedback from their experiences and through their internal and external relationships. This feedback is sent back up to the leadership team and incorporated into its next strategic review. This cycle continues until it's time for the leadership team to do its next visioning, which will, of course, include all feedback received to date.

At the top of the organization is an executive cycle that, once put into action, leads to a cycle that has no real end.

It's a continuous cycle of aligned communication and feedback that permeates all corners and pockets of the organization. Figure 14 depicts a simplified representation of the executive planning cycle, in which your organization's executives introspect, plan, and execute the strategy. This model can be used for any type of planning activities that begin at the executive level. It also helps explain the horizontal alignment process.

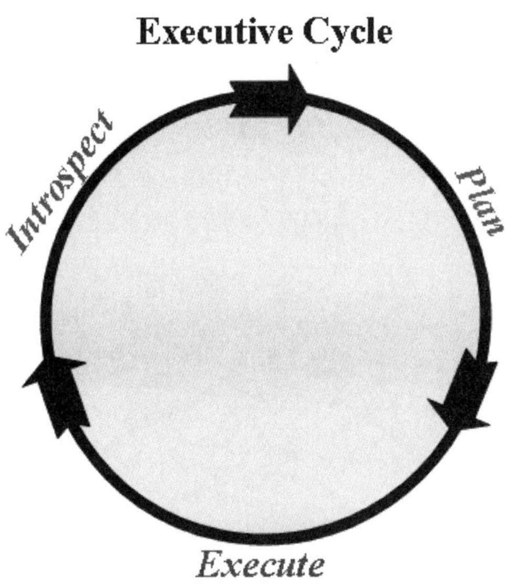


Figure 14. The Executive Planning Cycle

As we can see, after the executive team conceives ideas for change, its high-level plans are initiated and pushed on to execution. Once they are carried out, the executive team reviews the results in a debriefing session (or sessions) and develops new ideas based on the lessons learned from the initial implementation. Working collaboratively at each stage along the way keeps the executive team aligned and in sync when related decisions, or even new executive-level initiatives, are introduced. Members of the team are less likely to compete for resources and funding because they have a stake in the initiative at hand and have committed to their peers to see it through.

While this is an effective means of maintaining alignment at the executive level, we know through experience that the executives themselves will delegate the actual execution of the initiative down to the operational level. In figure 15 we see the interactions between the executive and the operational levels that are necessary to maintain vertical alignment at all stages of a strategic initiative.

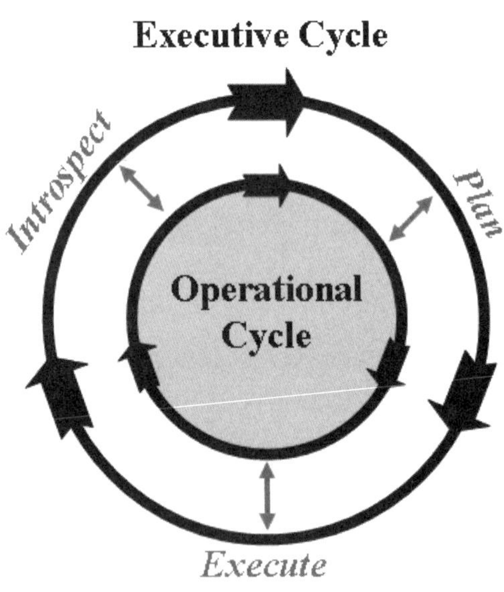


Figure 15. The Embedded Alignment Cycle

This embedded alignment cycle demonstrates how the action teams working at the operational level can be brought into the process at any stage to offer insights and feedback, and the program management office serves as the catalyst for communication between both cycles. The actions may require several different projects, working either simultaneously or sequentially, that all go through the same cycle, if perhaps more frequently than at the executive level.

Although executive meetings should take place every month or so, operational teams should meet on a weekly, or even a daily basis to introspect, plan, and execute. In this case introspection largely takes the form of reviewing the various phases of an initiative. Feedback is collected each time the operational teams meet and then presented to the executive team at its next meeting. The executive team uses this new information to make any necessary adjustments to the charter and also passes it along to the operational teams.

While a process like the embedded alignment cycle might seem very elementary, you need to ask yourself whether or not you're actually practicing this level of coordination in all areas of your business. Some may indeed have a strategic project underway in which project teams are working and meeting with a steering committee on a regular basis. But is this the norm? In my experience, it is not the norm, unless strictly mandated by policy. Daily operational routines and agendas tend to keep these meetings from happening, unless compliance is enforced at the top.

Other initiatives may be taking place in your organization today, such as implementing a new reporting tool or R&D collaboration process, or even introducing new shop-floor machinery that will increase productivity in the plant. Do all such strategic, high-value initiatives share a uniform process of horizontal alignment at the top that maintains alignment with and across all operational teams? If you cannot answer yes, your organization may not be ready to handle the number of new initiatives that could come with the fifth and final ring.

Both horizontal and vertical alignment must become the norm, not the exception. Your organization's culture must be one of deep introspection and sharing across all levels. Because the degree of compliance with the embedded alignment cycle differs drastically from one organization to the next, and even within a single organization, it may be necessary to conduct a change readiness and communication assessment. This will help you spot areas of potential communication breakdown and to develop a compulsory policy and process for communications and feedback across your company. Such a study is an inexpensive, very worthwhile investment in preparing your organization for a lifetime of continuous positive change.

I have stressed the need for communication and collaboration because they are critical elements in your organization's infrastructure as well as prerequisites for achieving the level of strategic excellence that the Fifth Ring Strategy has to offer. I have also highlighted other crucial elements that will allow your organization to become fluid and adaptable. But if your organization has long had a rigid hierarchical structure, how can you change it?

Fortunately, there is a quick and effective way to generate collaboration, even in some of the most rigid hierarchical structures.

## From Value Chain to Value Ring

Figure 16 shows what is known as "the generic value chain." It describes the increasing value that goods and services have as they move from one end of the value chain (left) to the other (right) and get closer and closer to the customer (outside right).

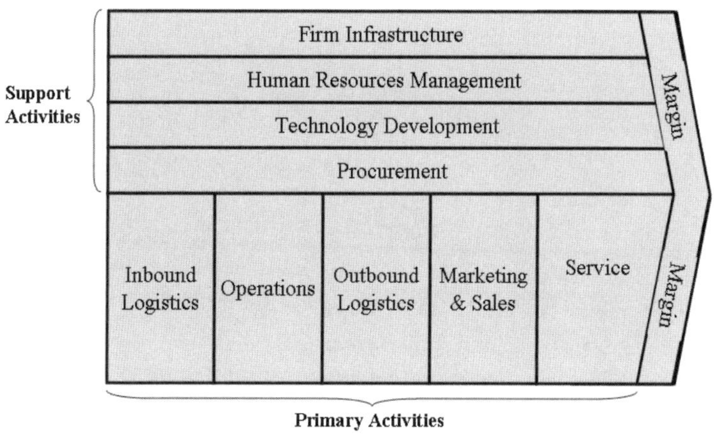


Figure 16. The Generic Value Chain

Michael Porter's value chain model has taught us a lot. For two decades, it has provided us with a very useful way to understand the activities that generate value in organizations. It has also enabled us to design an organization around the movement of goods and services to bring it maximum value.

But with the recent introduction of integrated management tools—such as enterprise resource planning (ERP), customer relationship management (CRM), supplier relationship management (SRM) and product lifecycle management (PLM) systems—it's now possible for your organization to achieve a much higher level of value. You can do this by converting the value chain to a value ring.

In figure 17 we see the continuous cycle of research and development, supply-chain, and demand-chain activities all feeding each other with the current and relevant information needed for improvement.

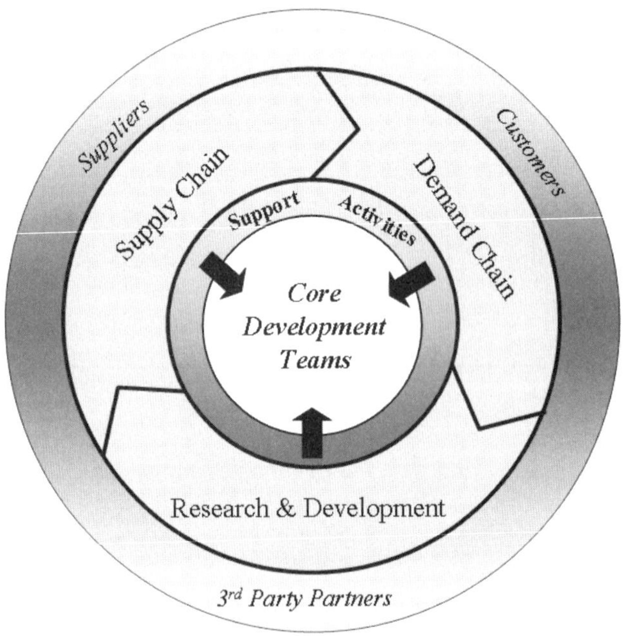


Figure 17. The Value Ring

The value ring has an inner circle of core development teams surrounded by support activities and then enveloped in borders containing the core work streams of research and development, the supply chain, and the demand chain. If we compare this model with the traditional value chain, we can easily recognize the potential organizational assignments.

Table 1. Organizational Elements of the Value Ring

| Core Entity | Organizational Elements |
|---|---|
| Research & Development | § New product discovery<br>§ New product development<br>§ Clinical development (life sciences companies)<br>§ New product engineering |
| Supply Chain | § Raw material purchasing<br>§ Inbound logistics<br>§ Inventory management<br>§ Manufacturing<br>§ Outbound logistics<br>§ Staffing (for fee-related services rendered)<br>§ Finance (controlling) |
| Demand Chain | § Warehouse management<br>§ Marketing<br>§ Sales<br>§ Customer service<br>§ Finance (pricing, invoicing) |

| Core Entity | Organizational Elements |
|---|---|
| Support Activities | § Information services<br>§ Human resources/human capital management<br>§ Non-raw materials purchasing<br>§ Finance (payables, receivables, reporting)<br>§ Strategic development |

You don't necessarily need to change the structure of your organization to adopt this model. However, it does require you to mobilize key individuals in support activities and each work stream to collaborate and work with your organization's other work streams.

For example, research and development could sponsor a core development team that would include individuals from sales, marketing, finance, engineering, and human resources to discuss such items as product viability, new market potential, customer demands, pricing, set-up costs, and core competency requirements with regard to a new product idea. This will give them the guidance they need to decide to continue, alter, or even stop a new product or service idea. In addition to internal resources, the core development teams can bring in suppliers, third-party partners, and even customers to help plan and design new initiatives.

## A Case In Point

I once consulted a large healthcare company that was able to reduce its new product pipeline from twenty-four months to fourteen, and save a significant amount of money and human resource time in the process. This monumental achievement was solely the result of designing and establishing a collaborative product lifecycle management process based on the Value Ring concept. Extended collaboration also allowed the sales and marketing groups to communicate the anticipated improvements to the marketplace in a timelier and more effective way.

In turn, the manufacturing plants were able to anticipate their production requirements and timing more accurately, thereby saving them a considerable amount of money up front, as well as on an ongoing basis. This healthcare manufacturer was able to set up and implement this process using collaborative teams extracted from various departments across their existing hierarchical organization. They were able to pull this off long before they were capable of making the process, organizational, and information systems changes that would provide a more permanent solution.

By now I'm sure you realize how crucial continual strategic change is to your organization's survival and how the rhythms and timing of such changes can either work significantly for you or against you, depending upon whether or not you evaluate and implement them properly. Even minor changes in your organization, which you can introduce with little effort, can have a major impact on your ability to thrive on rapid change, increase your visibility and collaboration, and add to the quality of your products and services. Such changes will also contribute to a happier and more self-actualized workforce by doing away with isolation, fragmentation, and compartmentalization of human thought.

Implementing the principles of Musashi's first four rings allows you to simultaneously focus on excellence in each of the strategic areas presented in figure 18. By allowing the channels of creativity to flow in all areas of your organization, you prepare it to achieve excellence in more than one strategic area.

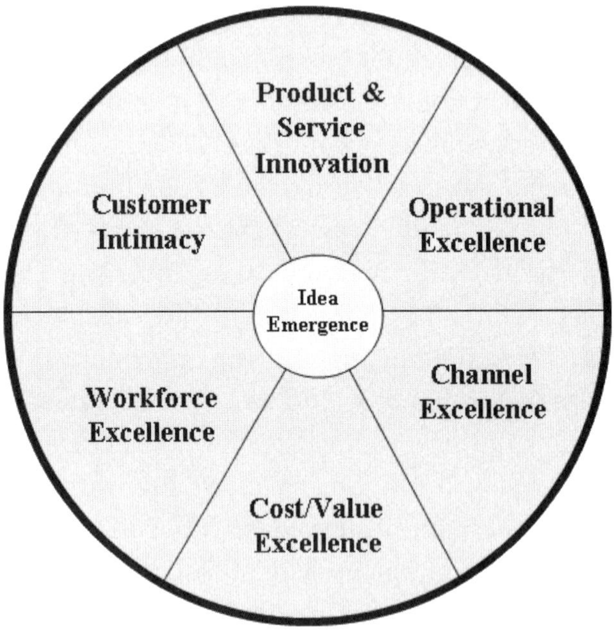


Figure 18: Wheel of Strategic Focus

Imagine, for example, that your competitors are battling it out, spending lots of capital to catch up with or surpass your company's new innovative product. Suddenly, with minor changes to your product, you're able to introduce a new channel for marketing and distribution that creates a whole new market segment never before tapped by anyone in your industry. Now you're not only at the top of the fitness landscape, but you're light years ahead of everyone else. They will never be able to catch up to your product *and* marketing capabilities—that is, unless you become complacent.

While your competitors were allocating many of their available resources to play catch-up, your organization had every spoke of its wheel of strategic focus churning out new ways to get closer to its shared vision. It didn't settle for a mindset of lack or limitation. Rather, it embraced one of abundance and possibility. And while the other companies were sweating out the heat of competitive battle, each of your individual employees was having fun and self-actualizing by becoming best in class in their respective work areas.

• • •

## Tips for Small Companies and Nonprofits

The fitness landscape most likely explains how your organization first came into existence. You conceived a unique idea that put you on top of an entirely new peak. Beware! No organization stays on the top of a peak unless it changes and adapts.

As soon as you come up with a new idea, begin to ponder how and when it should evolve and improve over time. Also begin to consider how your single product or service can migrate into a family of products and services so that related and complementary elements can add to its value. Talk to your customers and business partners to determine what your customers' next likely needs will be.

At the early stages of your organization's growth, avoid the traditional hierarchical organizational model and value chain. Organizing around the value ring will ultimately provide your organization with more flexibility and responsiveness. Furthermore, you will avoid the headaches that many larger organizations, having grown up around a more linear model, find extremely difficult to change.

• • •

Now that you've mastered the first four rings, you're ready to move on to the final level of strategic development—Emptiness—the enlightened state that will usher your company into a new era of continuous growth and prosperity.

# Part III

# Adopting the Fifth Ring Strategy

IF YOU'VE DILIGENTLY WORKED your way through Musashi's first four rings in chapters 4 through 7, you now have a solid foundation for your organization. You've created an environment conducive to strategic excellence, and you're ready to adopt the integrated planning process of the Fifth Ring Strategy. You're at a critical turning point. You're about to move into the realm of what Musashi calls Emptiness.

Imagine your next strategic planning session. Instead of finding ways to cut manufacturing energy costs, you come up with a revolutionary new technology that not only eliminates those costs, but actually spawns a whole new industry from which you profit. Instead of finding ways to take back a segment of the market from your competitors, you create the next big trend that brings customers knocking on your door, leaving the old segment irrelevant or obsolete. These are the kind of results you can expect from implementing the Fifth Ring Strategy.

Chapter 8 is the very core of this book. The application of the principles of Emptiness is what makes *Breaking the Musashi Code* different from all other approaches for organizational strategy. Here you will learn how to master the art of visioning in an organizational setting of any size, shape, or focus. The remaining chapters show step-by-step how to create a vision and make it a reality in your organization.

Adopting the Fifth Ring Strategy as a governing metaprocess in your organization is exciting—even fun!—and your employees, your customers, your shareholders, and your competitors will all wonder what happened to your organization as it moves into an untouchable class of its own.

## Chapter 8

# Emptiness: Mastering the Art of Visioning

In the Book of Emptiness, Musashi explains how nothing ever simply "is," but is instead, always "becoming." This means that if you view your organization as it is today, and do not view it as infinite possibility like a blank canvas, it will remain in a constant state of stability. Stability in this context means "I don't have to react to changes," or "I won't have to develop anything new," or, worse yet, "I won't have to learn anything new." And, as we have seen in Chapter 2, stability eventually leads to organizational death.

For some, stability seems to provide a false sense of security. In reality though, stability never really means the absence of change, for the moment you begin to believe that things are stable, forced changes become inevitable. Obsolescence, turnover, competitive threats, shareholder issues, and customer dynamics—just to name a few—are always creating disturbances and keeping you in reactive motion, whether you want to believe it or not. If you choose not to react to these forces, your organization will begin to fall apart from the outside-in. Stability is just an illusion for those who fail to realize that change is inevitable.

Accepting that things are always "becoming" is the beginning of a lifelong relationship with visionary strategy. Knowing that there can be no absence of change leaves you three choices, each one of which will lead to an entirely different outcome:

1. You can choose to do nothing. (By now you know where this will lead you!)
2. You can choose to react to changes that will occur in your sphere of influence.
3. You can choose to be the creator and driver of change in your sphere of influence.

The choice is so simple, yet its ramifications so profound. To choose not to change or to merely react to change will condemn your organization to mediocrity or eventual disintegration. Being the creator and driver of change, on the other hand, will free you from perceptions of lack and limitation and leave you free to choose, free to create, and free to succeed.

Believing that events in your organization are always "becoming" changes the way you think about strategic planning and management. Strategic planning is no longer merely something that occurs every few years when the need arises. It's an ongoing, proactive process or mindset within your organization that continuously drives new visionary ideas and change. Figure 19 depicts the integrated planning process of the Fifth Ring Strategy.

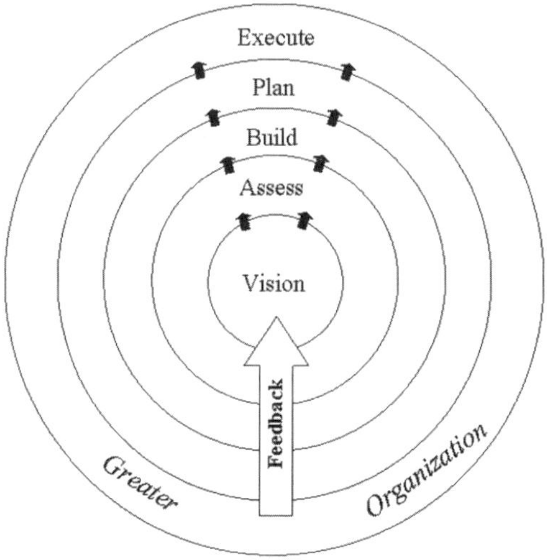


Figure 19. The Integrated Planning Process

Stability is anathema to all phases of the integrated planning process. If you allow a mindset of stability, your workforce, including your senior management team, will begin to long for it, strive for it, and eventually find excuses to obtain more and more of it by running to their routine operational processes for cover. Therefore, you need to remove the idea of stability once and for all and never allow it to resurface in the strategic planning process. The Fifth Ring Strategy is a meta-process without a definitive end. It's a continual recycling and improvement that drives continuous change and growth.

"No stability" doesn't imply that employees will have to work harder without breaks, or that they will be chained to their desks for a life of brutally punishing labor. In fact, it means something altogether different. It simply means maintaining the momentum of continuous strategic change. Provided that job descriptions and work tasks are assigned appropriately and fairly, employees will have time to vision, think, plan, and pioneer new areas for your organization's continued growth and prosperity. This is much different than stability. When given this type of work, employees tend to feel more valued and self-actualized, and that motivates them to take charge and work in a more productive and responsible manner. Their focus expands from ongoing work cycles to ongoing creativity and development, both at a personal and an organizational level.

This is an environment in which your organization, if given the proper guidance and direction, will continuously thrive. Eventually it will surpass the capabilities of competitors stuck in the old ways of thinking and managing their business. Guiding and directing it properly begins with the *vision core* of the Fifth Ring Strategy (figure 20). At the heart of this strategy is knowing not only what steps to take to develop a set of new visionary strategies for your organization, but also how to turn them into actionable goals or intentions.

The rest of this chapter is dedicated to guiding you through the strategic visioning retreat, which is the pivotal point at which most strategic change originates. Experiences from successful past visioning retreats are shared, outlining helpful tips and details to ensure that your retreat is the best that it can be.

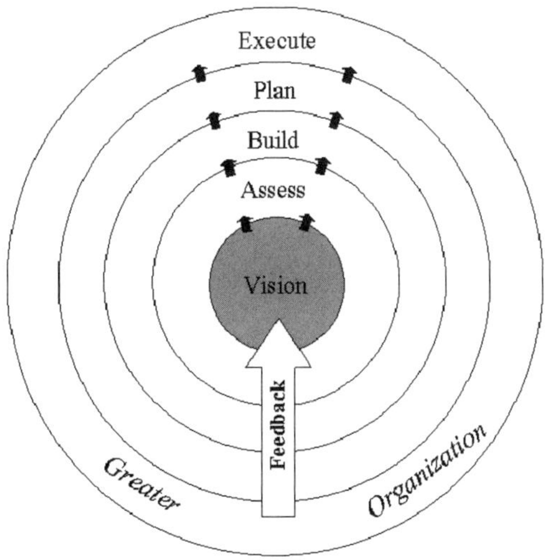


Figure 20. The Visioning Core of the Fifth Ring Strategy

## Planning the Visioning Retreat

Before you send out invitations, plan your strategic visioning retreat. You want to make sure that the right people show up with the right attitudes, fully prepared to work collaboratively. Proper planning will mitigate the risk that participants will misunderstand the objectives, not prepare, or simply not show up.

As the old carpenter's saying goes, "Measure twice, and cut once." It's important to get it right the first time because, given the busy schedules and time limitations of most executives today, you might not get another chance. You'll want to take full advantage of the opportunities provided by pulling this much horsepower into play at a single point in time. Planning will allow you to achieve the greatest results possible by leveraging the knowledge and synergies of your entire executive management team.

## Deciding Who Needs to Attend

The first question in the planning process is "Who needs to be there?" Based on my experience, I believe that pulling representatives from your entire business *system* will yield the greatest results. Representatives of the various business areas should be the top-level personnel. These are the people with the greatest insight and oversight in their respective areas, and they are empowered to make decisions about its future direction. Here are some examples of who should be included in the visioning retreats of various kinds of organizations.

### *A Holding Company*

A holding company would include, at minimum, the company's entire "C-level" (CEO, CFO, COO, and CIO), the CEOs or presidents from each major subsidiary, and the VP or general manager of any shared-service organizations. This will ensure that representatives of all major business areas of the holding company are present to discuss any ideas that emerge in the session.

### *A Large Multidivisional Company or Subsidiary*

Large multidivisional units and subsidiaries of holding companies develop their own strategies independently and are considered autonomous. Such organizations will want to invite, at minimum, the entire C-level of the organization, all division general managers, the VP of human resources, and any other major department that supports the entire company. The only difference between a multidivisional company and a subsidiary is that the subsidiary needs to invite an executive representative from the parent company to ensure that the emerging vision is in alignment with the corporate-level vision. If you have any questions about whether or not the right people are being invited, simply ask yourself, "Is the entire organization, including any major profit and cost center, represented?"

### *A Division or Department*

A divisional visioning retreat is focused primarily on developing strategies for business units or departments (Information Services or Human Resources, for example), as opposed to corporate strategies. Therefore, all divisional or departmental units that maintain autonomous operations will need to be represented, as well as any corporate functions.

For instance, if a division has its own sales force but relies on corporate marketing, division managers will need to invite both their divisional sales head and a representative of the corporate marketing group. As with a subsidiary, a divisional or business-unit strategy will need to include a mix of all representatives of all major business and support functions that contribute to the success of the division, whether from within the division or from the corporate office.

### A Small Business

Small businesses have one thing that clearly differentiates them from their larger counterparts: limited resources. This means they will have to conduct their visioning in a much more organic fashion and include most, if not all, members of the organization. The members of a small business organization, who are often just the owners, will have to wear several different hats throughout the strategic planning and implementation lifecycle.

In a mom-and-pop shop, for example, the mom may be responsible for managing the finances, business partnerships, and suppliers, while the pop might be in charge of day-to-day business operations. Both will need to bring their multifaceted perspectives to the table during the visioning retreat. Slightly larger companies may choose to include some key, if not all, employees of their business to ensure that the entire system is represented.

### A Nonprofit

Nonprofits, while somewhat different than most commercial organizations, still need to represent their system in its entirety. The majority of nonprofit organizations are community-based operations that have a very broad-ranging constituency for their size. If they are small, the board of directors will typically be a *hands-on* board. Along with other key volunteers from the community, it supports the organization's mission through activities such as committee work, fundraising, and filling in operational gaps when needed. Therefore, smaller nonprofits should always include the board of directors, the executive director, and the managing (if not all) staff members responsible for the individual services offered by the organization.

Community-based nonprofits will sometimes include others who are important to the success of their organization. Some examples might be founders, former board members, key donors, city officials, and even clientele who have received services from the organization. Larger regional, state, and national nonprofits will include the board of directors, but will often limit participation to the executive director, regional directors, service-line directors, and directors of major support functions like human resources and information services.

Be careful not to invite too many people from every corner of your organization if it is large. Not only is it difficult to manage a group of more than about forty to fifty participants, but there may also be a tendency for non-executives to jump into the operational details. If this happens, you could lose the intended strategic focus.

## Generating Ideas

There are several reasons why it's important to have all areas of the organization represented in the room for the visioning exercise.

### *Mutual Learning*

A visioning retreat provides an optimal environment for the senior members of your organization to learn from one another. You see, the visioning retreat isn't just for planning purposes. It's also a significant opportunity for all who attend to learn what their peers are doing and to provide feedback from the perspective of their own area of responsibility. In the process, they not only come up with new ideas for themselves, but also realize that they can operate more effectively by acting in unison with their counterparts. As a result, all participants gain a more holistic perspective of their organization and are prepared to make better decisions on a day-to-day basis.

### *Mutual Teaching*

If learning is one side of the coin, teaching is the other. Over the past several decades there's been a lot said about learning organizations. As participants discuss their ideas and the value they will bring to their respective areas of the organization, they become effective teachers who can foster a self-sustaining environment of continuous learning without the need for overly bureaucratic controls and processes.

### *Mutual Accountability*

Mutual accountability is much more likely to be achieved when the executives who make key decisions look one another in the eyes as they commit to these decisions. Agreeing to a strategy without having been in the room as it was being developed always leaves room for executives to withdraw support from it, either because of some misunderstanding, or simply by withdrawing support because they were not involved in the process. Having them all in the room together when strategy is developed and giving them all ample opportunity to question, alter, and craft an idea together eliminates the possibility that they will withdraw their support in the future.

### *Leveraging Ideas*

In a group setting where executives are teaching and learning from one another, one executive will often express an idea similar to one that another executive has been pondering for some time. When the first executive brings the idea to the forefront for discussion, the second then steps in with new ideas. This creates a synergy that leads to an improved solution.

For example, the general manager of one division might state her idea for developing a customer relationship management process that will improve customer intelligence so her product division can create demand instead of continuously reacting to ever-changing customer demand. As this is being discussed, another general manager from another product division tells her that he has been considering something similar but wants this information to be fed to the marketing department for more effective targeting. As these two leverage each other's ideas, the chief information officer jumps in and explains how an enterprise-wide customer relationship management (CRM) systems solution would allow both divisions to do what they need, as well as provide improved reporting and analytic capabilities at both the divisional and corporate levels. This type of leveraging experience is far more likely to occur in an environment where representatives from the entire system are present.

## Allocating the Time

Once you've determined who will need to attend the visioning retreat, you'll need to fix a time when all participants can come together at an off-site location for one to three days. The rule of thumb is to allocate one full day for a small business or nonprofit and two days for a larger company that has already determined and doesn't wish to review its core values, mission statement, lifecycle position, or opportunity analysis.

Three days are typically required for larger organizations that want to review all foundational materials, perform the visioning, and prioritize their new strategies. This may seem like a lot of time to some, and there will always be a few who say they can't set aside that much time for a visioning retreat because they have too much other important work to do. In such cases, I challenge the organizational leadership team by asking them what could be more important than determining the future of their organization. I rarely lose this argument.

## Finding the Right Location

The final step in planning for the visioning retreat is to determine the right location for the event. Location is a very important element in the planning process for several reasons.

### *To Reduce Distractions*

One of the main objectives in holding the visioning retreat off-site is to remove the participants from the distractions of their daily work routines, their families, and their free-time activities. While some distractions are less intrusive than others, you should avoid all of them if possible. This will allow the participants to focus their full attention on developing new strategy. If one distraction is allowed, it will eventually lead to another, and then another. Soon each participant will be stepping out of the session to take phone calls and attend meetings. If developing the new strategy isn't important enough to avoid such distractions for a few days, your organization has larger issues to attend to, and you should put the event on hold until all can be fully present.

### *To Inspire New Ideas*

The off-site setting should be an aesthetic one that provides quiet spaces and secluded paths where the participants can walk around before and after sessions and during breaks to let their minds become clear and focused. Contrary to the popular corporate belief that continuous doing and thinking stimulate progress, emptying the mind is what allows innovative thoughts to emerge. This cannot happen when the mind is full of daily thoughts and concerns.

While most corporate executives are reluctant to practice meditation or any other sort of mind-emptying exercise, I do find nearly all of them walking about at some point during the session in a quiet, reflective state, enjoying the natural settings and peaceful environment and allowing their rational minds to rest. When they return to their group of peers who have been doing the same thing, it's amazing to see the new ideas that have broken through and how the energy in the room shifts from the facilitator to the participants.

### *To Build Group Cohesiveness*

As you'll recall, in chapter 2 I discussed the dynamics of the legitimate and shadow systems. These two systems, which are present in all organizations, consistently challenge each other. One provides the structure, while the other circumvents and challenges the structure in a continuous attempt to communicate through channels that are restricted by formality. A visioning retreat is one of the rare occasions when an organization's formal and shadow systems can come together, strengthen each other, and find new legitimate pathways for visionary ideas to permeate the organization, both horizontally and vertically.

An off-site visioning retreat also gives executives time to network and deepen their relationships. Providing a team-building activity on the first day and restricting out-of-session activities to meals will give participants adequate time to mingle and discuss events of the day and relate them to their respective areas of responsibility. When participants are kept on site for the entire two- to three-day session, networking and interaction will increase with each new day.

## Preparing for the Visioning Retreat

As the time for the visioning retreat approaches, you'll need to update key documents, find a good facilitator, and get the conference room ready.

As you prepare for the visioning retreat, you'll need to update the documents that you used to achieve the Earth and Water levels in your organization. In order to save valuable executive time, you should prepare as many of these documents as possible before the visioning retreat. For example, the finance team can perform the financial and risk analyses and plot the company in the proper life-cycle quadrant. Environmental and social sustainability reports can be generated, showing the current programs and outstanding risk status in these areas. An opportunity analysis questionnaire can be distributed and the results collected and published prior to the main event. At a minimum, the following documents should be completed and ready to support the visioning retreat when it begins.

### *Vision and Mission Statements*

The vision and mission statements serve as the primary filters for all visionary ideas, goals, and strategies generated during the session. Therefore, they will need to be posted in plain view in the room where the visioning will take place. They serve as a grounding mechanism to keep everyone within the same strategic parameters and provide a way to easily weed out ideas, goals, and strategies that don't align with the vision or mission.

If, for some reason, your organization doesn't yet have a

clear vision and mission statement, you'll need to take time at the beginning of the session for the group to discuss and generate the core criteria for the vision and mission. Never assume that these can be completed and agreed upon in one day. It takes time and careful crafting to complete these tell-all statements. The focus should be on identifying and agreeing upon the main criteria for these statements. That will be enough to continue the visioning retreat.

### *Core Values*

Core values are also used as a filtering mechanism for the visionary goals and objectives. If any ideas generated aren't in alignment with the core values, you should consider eliminating them. If your organization hasn't yet identified and published its core values, you'll need to plan for some kind of exercise to ensure that the core values are clearly defined before the visioning proceeds.

As with the vision and mission statements, this will take more that a day to complete, so it would probably be a better use of your time to capture an initial list of values using some form of appreciative inquiry technique (see Chapter 4) prior to the visioning retreat. Appreciative inquiry will not only help you identify your core values, but also serve as an effective icebreaker to get participants out of their heads and into their hearts.

### *Key Financial Trends and Analysis*

Financial reports should be prepared and reviewed prior to the visioning exercise to ground the participants in the history of the organization, its current state, and where it is likely headed. Designing a financial trending report is more of an art than a science. An effective one will paint a picture not only of your organization's past and present, but also its probable future if it continues on its present course. Risk management reports should also be included, including the company's environmental and social sustainability and awareness levels and existing programs.

It's important that all participants get the same information about the organization's position, the issues it is struggling with, and the potential pitfalls it faces in the future. Such information equips the executive visioning team to understand both the challenges and opportunities visionary ideas will present.

### *Strategic Lifecycle Chart*

Your organization's position in the strategic lifecycle chart should be carefully plotted by the finance team and displayed in the visioning conference room. By seeing how the company is maturing, participants can adopt a strategic direction that will bolster its chances for success in the future. Similar to financial trends analysis, the opportunity analysis, and the vision and mission statements, the strategic lifecycle chart educates all participants about the realities of your organization's current position. Such knowledge serves as a filter for ideas that aren't in alignment with that position and justifies eliminating them from further consideration.

### *Opportunity Analysis*

The opportunity analysis is one of the most useful elements in grounding the executive visioning team in the current state of the organization, and the entire group should contemplate and discuss each segment. Unlike the financial trends analysis and the strategic lifecycle chart, the opportunity analysis provides a more detailed view into the current state of the organization and gives participants a more in-depth knowledge of its environment. This knowledge of self, as well as of outside threats and relationships, will help participants determine the opportunistic strategies they will need to be successful given their current strengths, weaknesses and threats.

## Finding the Right Facilitator

The person chosen to facilitate the visioning session shouldn't be from among the executive visioning participants, as he or she will need to adhere to a position of complete and uncompromised neutrality. The facilitator will need to review and fully understand all of the preliminary documents discussed, as well as the implications of each document for the future of the organization.

After carefully studying every possible opportunity within every department regarding every competitive threat, weakness, strength, and relationship, an effective facilitator will craft a series of visioning scenarios to guide participants through a visualization exercise in which thought-provoking questions will stimulate visions of the organization's future in the minds of the participants.

Crafting visioning scenarios is a key element in preparing for a successful visioning exercise. These questions can lead either to a highly successful visionary outcome or to a less-than-desirable outcome, depending on the care put into their creation. A skilled facilitator will know how to craft questions that will get the participants outside of their current mindset. He or she will know how to help them relax and empty their minds of intrusive thoughts so they can envision their organization's future when the time comes.

### *Preparing the Room*

All props must be visible to everyone in the room. Chairs should be arranged in a semicircle, or "U" shape so that each participant has all the others in plain view. The facilitator will be at the opening of the semicircle seating arrangement, with the flipcharts and one large segment of wall in clear sight of everyone. The wall should be covered with a large sheet of paper that will be used for brainstorming after the visioning is complete. The room should be comfortable and relaxing, with plenty of space for participants to walk around, stretch their legs, and get refreshments from the back of the room. Keep in mind that such sessions are long and often exhausting, so be sure to provide plenty of snacks and beverages. Once the room is prepared, and the team has been updated on all of the preparatory reports, charts and opportunities, the visioning exercise can begin.

## Conducting the Visioning Session

If the visioning session goes well, great ideas will emerge. But if it isn't conducted properly, it will end up like any other strategic planning session. Incremental ideas and changes will be the outcome of the day. To be successful, a visioning session needs to be based on Musashi's principles of Emptiness, which is closely aligned with the non-linear principle of "emergence" discussed in Chapter 2.

### *Start with Emptiness*

Emptiness, in Eastern philosophical context, simply means achieving an enlightened state within the conscious mind—or in the case of organizations, the *collective* conscious mind.

Some executives may resist visioning because they feel that they have all of the answers in their heads. The problem with this is that they are normally so busy that they rarely have time to think things through, much less spend the quiet time needed to allow bold new ideas to emerge from a higher state of inner awareness. This is much different than when our rational brains produce an idea, which is usually a derivative of our experiences, emotions, or existing thoughts—which is to say that it isn't bold at all.

Those executives who know they don't have all the answers often want to pull in an outside "expert" to tell them how to run their business. But when they pull in outside firms to plan their strategies, they end up benchmarking the organization against others who are experiencing the same problems they are. The result is usually just a different form of mediocrity, which I call *industry homogenization*. Furthermore, these experts don't know your specific markets, your customers' unique demands, your suppliers, or your channel partners, let alone your organization's unique culture.

For an outside firm to assume that it can enter an unknown organization and produce a sound strategy for it is the epitome of arrogance. This is why strategies developed by outside firms are often not put into action. Instead of *telling* their clients what they need to do, consultants need to be doing more *asking*, leading them with thought-provoking questions that force them out of their comfort zones.

If you spend the time necessary to keep your people educated in their respective fields, you must trust that somewhere deep inside of each participant lies those hidden ideas that will ultimately create major breakthroughs for your organization. Isn't this why they were hired in the first place?

### *Establish the Right Rules*

Before starting the session on the first day, I like to go over the rules of engagement. Setting some expectations ensures that the session remains on track and that all participants feel encouraged to speak up as equals. The rules are quite simple and include the following:

- Turn off all distracters like phones and laptops.
- Leave your title at the door.
- Trust the process, allowing the facilitator to guide you through it.
- Treat everyone with respect and listen to what each

participant has to say.

- Question with curiosity, not judgment.
- Provide direct, yet constructive feedback whenever it is warranted.
- Receive feedback with an open mind and without defensiveness.
- Realize that there are no stupid questions.
- Create a parking lot for important non-related issues that arise so they can be resolved after the visioning retreat.
- Participate in each exercise with full enthusiasm.

I like to spend a bit more time discussing that last rule. Some executives I've worked with don't initially feel comfortable letting go of their rational thoughts and allowing themselves to enter that quiet space where creative ideas are born. I explain to them the reasons for using the creative visioning process instead of more conventional means. I also provide them with a few success stories to establish credibility. I then ask each participant to make a commitment to follow the rules and the process. It also helps when the sponsor of the visioning retreat (the CEO or highest-ranking executive) declares his or her support of the process.

### *Review of Background Materials*

Once everyone is on board, it's time to walk through the vision, mission, core values, and various analyses outlined earlier. When I facilitate a visioning retreat, I make sure to spend enough time on each document to thoroughly ground every participant in the material. That way, everyone in the group will share a common understanding of where the organization stands with regard to its position in the marketplace or its respective environment.

I explain to the participants how to use the material as filters for each idea brought forth during the session. I give them permission to stand up at any time, walk around the room, and review any piece of background material relevant to the discussion or exercise in progress. This review, which may take up to half a day to complete, ensures that all participants are of the same mindset regarding the organization's status.

## Carrying Out the Visioning Exercise

As a facilitator, I begin the actual visioning by quieting the participants and making sure they are comfortable and at ease. I encourage them to close their eyes, take a few deep breaths, sit on the floor, or do whatever is necessary to get them into a relaxed, yet aware state. When the room is completely still, I verbally guide them into a meditative state by having them let go of their busy thoughts. The goal is to get each of the participants to operate out of a heightened state of awareness, and that requires stillness and a mind devoid of any *mind chatter*.

### *Creating the Strategic Framework*

Once the participants have left their fast-paced, day-to-day state of mind behind and entered a state of *emptiness*, I introduce them to a scenario by quietly asking them to envision themselves waking up several years from now. I then begin to ask lead-in questions that allow them to actually *experience* their vision in the present moment, such as:

- You pick up the morning paper. What do the headlines say about your organization?
- You find an article about your organization. What does it say?
- You go to work. Where are you actually going?
- You see people along the way. What are they saying about your organization?
- You arrive at work. What does it look like?
- You walk in your building. What do you immediately feel?
- What do you notice about your workplace?
- Who is there? What are they doing?
- What is your organization doing at this time?
- What are your organization's products, services, or other activities?

During these general lead-in questions I pause after each question to allow the participants to sit with it for a while and write down all thoughts and ideas that come to mind. I then continue with more targeted questions that probe into areas of concern that have arisen through the opportunity and financial analyses. With a full range of representatives in the room, at least one, and quite often several, will come up with a breakthrough idea to satisfy an opportunity.

For example, if it has been determined through the opportunity analysis that the company's distribution channels are challenged by heavy competition that causes serious profit erosion, I might ask future-state questions such as:

- What distribution channels are we operating through in this future state?
- How have other divisions or subsidiaries been leveraged to achieve breakthroughs in the distribution process in this future state?
- What external alliances allowed for breakthroughs in distribution optimization?
- What are *you* doing differently that allowed this breakthrough to occur?

Using vision-evoking questions, I address each strategic business challenge and each strategic theme in every segment of the opportunity analysis. Then I pause to allow participants to explore and visualize emerging ideas and write down each one. Even though they may not grasp the full meaning of a thought that emerged at the time, they should still write it down, as it may make sense later.

It is up to the facilitator to come up with creative visioning and visualization scenarios that will explore the unknown territories that will allow the participants to ponder every opportunity. Such scenarios should be created with time and care, as they are one of the keys to successful visioning and breaking new ground. Each strategic area of the business should be explored, seeking out new visions that can catapult the business forward, away from the competitive state. Creative scenario development will guide participants outside of their proverbial *box*, allowing them to envision solutions that cross competency, departmental and even industry boundaries.

After the guided visioning exercise, I quietly instruct the

participants to remain in that frame of mind and to take some time, or even take a walk, while they continue to ponder the ideas they have written down. I ask them to avoid any outside disturbances for the next hour or so and not to talk with one another except to clarify or confirm a thought or idea they may have had. I encourage them to continue writing down their thoughts until it's time to return to the room.

When everyone has returned to the room, I ask them to review all of the ideas they wrote down and to choose the five or so that they consider the most significant based on their overall value to and impact on the organization. They should also assess each idea in light of the filters—vision, mission, core values, opportunity analysis, and lifecycle position—to ensure that they are appropriate for the organization. If more than 20 or so participants are in the room, I ask them to break out into groups of four or five to do this exercise.

Once all participants, or groups, have chosen their top five ideas, I ask them to write each one on an individual three-by-five inch sticky note. Then, I ask each participant, or group representative, to walk up to the front of the room, and stick each note, in no particular order, on the large paper backdrop that was previously hung on the wall. I ask them to do this *without* conversation. When everyone has done this, there should be one large random, unorganized grouping of sticky notes on the paper.

Next, I ask all participants to go up to the wall and, while holding conversation to a minimum, begin to group the sticky notes into themes. For example, if several ideas pertain to customer service, they should all be grouped together. If knowledge management is a theme, all sticky notes with ideas about it should be placed in the same group. No individual should be assigned to do the work on behalf of the others. Instead, the order should emerge from the entire group. However, it's important for each participant to look over the groupings and agree that all the sticky notes are in the right place.

After the last participant has reviewed the groupings and the entire group has agreed on them, the facilitator then walks through each one, reading the idea on each sticky note so the group can discuss it. As the group reviews each individual idea, I try to make sure that every participant thoroughly understands each idea. Taking the time for each individual to share and explain his or her idea generates new insights in their peers. As a result of such discussion, some new leveraging ideas may emerge, and they shouldn't be ignored. When this happens, I simply fill out another sticky note and put it in the proper grouping.

Giving everyone the opportunity to provide deep constructive feedback to those explaining their ideas can create a meaningful learning experience for each participant. This is what is known as *double-loop* learning. Such learning requires a willingness of each team member to openly reflect on past performance and to graciously receive constructive feedback from the other team members. Double-loop learning provides a highly effective means of teaching those who are always expected to have all the right answers, and who therefore don't always have the opportunity to become effective learners.

The process leads to deep personal introspection, and if facilitated with care, it can lead to more profound and longer-lasting results than any other form of training or knowledge sharing. If not facilitated with care, however, it can become a way for some to bolster their egos or flex their political muscle. This will ultimately lead to defensiveness and perhaps even permanently damage relationships—the exact opposite of what we are trying to achieve.

Some ideas may at first seem bold, if not outrageous at first. Nevertheless, the group needs to carefully consider and thoroughly discuss each one. I challenge participants who don't appear to take an idea seriously and ask the author of that idea to explain his or her thoughts so the group can fully explore the subject. Such out-of-the-box ideas are often the very ones that can transform an organization by bringing it out of its rut of mediocrity and complacency and landing it on the top of a new peak of the fitness landscape. This is the essence of what we are trying to achieve!

As the review proceeds, the group will most likely find that some ideas should have been put in a different grouping, or even that some groupings are redundant or overlapping and should be combined. When each grouping has been reviewed and finalized, I circle it and ask the participants to come up with an affirmative goal statement that represents it.

If the participants do this properly, they should end up with no more that four to six goal statements in all. If there are more that six, I ask the group to take time to evaluate each one again to determine if it represents a goal, or merely a critical success factor that could support one or more of the goals. If some of the groupings turn out to be critical success factors instead of goals, they are put aside until it's time to discuss critical success factors.

The final goal statements should be reviewed against the following *SAM* criteria:

- Are they *simple* enough for everyone in our organization to understand?
- Are they *attainable,* given our organization's capabilities and mission?
- Are they *measurable* so we can demonstrate progress and success within a specified period of time?

While the goal statement will likely not – and should not – be stated in quantifiable terms at the time it is created, caution should be given to ensure that performance measures can be applied to it at some point in the future. This SAM acronym is very easy to remember. If any goal statement doesn't meet these criteria, it should be revisited and either reconsidered or reworded until it does.

When the groupings have been agreed upon, the goal statements finalized, and each participant feels that he or she fully understands everything posted on the wall, the first day comes to an end. The results of the first day should remain on the wall. It's the strategic framework for the next day's activities, in which the group will devise strategic initiatives for each new goal.

## Developing the Strategic Initiatives

At the beginning of the second day, when all the participants are feeling refreshed, the group can begin to develop strategic initiatives to address each of the strategic goal statements. The goals provide the strategic framework for the various areas of the organization that require strategic attention, and the group will develop one or more strategic initiatives to support the realization of each goal.

Since strategic initiatives will emerge in all shapes and sizes, the numbers of resources required to achieve each one will vary greatly. Nothing should be excluded from the final list based on how time consuming or expensive it is. What's important is the value it will bring to the organization. Strategic value is defined in different ways by different organizations, but at a minimum, it includes the following:

- Contribution to shareholder or stakeholder value
- Positive public exposure
- Enhancement of the organization's image
- Vision and mission achievement
- Customer or constituent satisfaction

In order to develop strategic initiatives for each goal statement, the group will need to revisit each individual idea on the sticky notes on a goal-by-goal basis. The individual ideas posted during the visioning session should not automatically become strategic initiatives. Rather, they should be viewed collectively as guidelines within which new ideas for strategic initiatives will emerge.

The group should discuss each grouping and determine what strategic initiatives will be necessary to achieve a given goal. Some initiatives will already appear in each grouping of sticky notes, but other ideas should emerge through discussion. This will allow the group to carefully craft the strategic initiatives needed to support the goal. If too many initiatives are developed, the group should look at each one to see if should be merged into another initiative. If the group gets stuck on an issue, you can do another short visioning session that focuses on the question at hand.

There shouldn't be more than four or five initiatives per goal statement when finished. (Don't worry—there will be plenty of opportunity to develop subordinate projects under each strategic initiative.) The goals and their supporting strategic initiatives should then be written up in a concise, yet meaningful manner. Figure 21 shows an example of a single strategic goal statement with its supporting strategic initiatives. Of course, several such goal statements will be written up, depending on how many the group generated during the visioning.

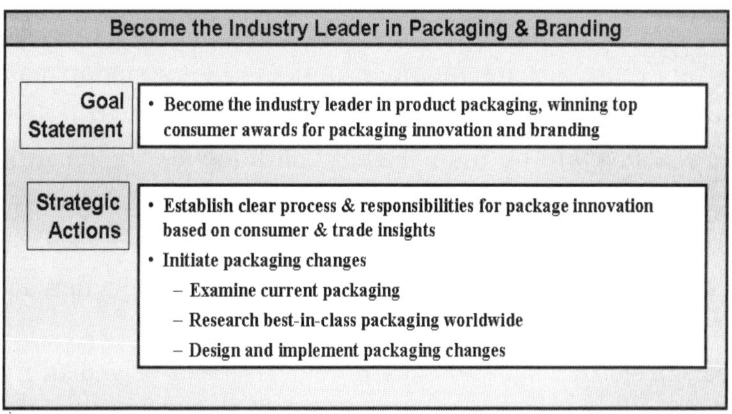


Figure 21. Sample Goal Statement and Supporting Initiatives

Participants should refrain from trying to add more detail and description at this point. There are a couple of reasons for this. First, simplicity is the key to effective communication, and the strategic goals will need to be communicated to all levels of the organization, as well as to shareholders, for them to be most effective. Second, adding too much detail will reduce the creativity put into the process of implementing the initiatives and achieving the goals.

For example, if we were to leave the statement as it reads in figure 21 and then pass it down as is to the team we later select to implement that goal, the team will have much more creative license to come up with new ideas and innovative breakthroughs. In addition, the team will be much closer to the underlying issues that necessitated the goal and much more likely to have the expertise to provide a more innovative solution. By adding too much detail and structure, the executive team essentially shuts down the minds of those most capable of meeting the challenge.

For their part, the members of the implementation team would be left to drone through the detailed instructions provided them by their leaders, perhaps feeling disgruntled because they have a better solution but aren't allowed to implement it. It's much better to pass down strategic guidelines to the team and allow it to develop the detailed descriptions and plans of what to do and how to do it. The executive management team will still be involved in the review and approval process and will be able to veto any ideas that aren't aligned with the intention they had when they developed the goal.

## Determining Critical Success Factors and Core Competencies

Once the goal statements and underlying strategic initiatives have been completed and agreed upon, it's time to determine critical success factors and core competencies on a goal-by-goal basis. This can be achieved either by applying the sticky note method I described earlier, or simply through group discussion. The main objective is to identify the critical success factors and core competencies that require strategic attention because they don't yet exist in your organization. If they did exist, the goals could be achieved by business as usual.

Critical success factors are those elements that must be added, removed, or changed in order for your organization to achieve its stated goal. For example, if the goal statement is to "achieve top ranking in an independent, industry-wide customer satisfaction survey," the critical success factor might be the need for better customer intelligence. If the goal statement is to "develop a first-class supply chain that can be outsourced to other companies," the critical success factor might be improved visibility and tracking capabilities in all areas of the supply chain. In both cases, each critical success factor would likely become either a strategic initiative that directly supports the goal, or a separate tactical initiative that falls under one of the strategic initiatives. Either way, the critical success factor becomes an important part of achieving the goal.

Core competencies are similar to critical success factors in that they also support a strategic goal. In fact, a core competency can become a strategic initiative. I've done some work with small, emerging biotech companies that are still in their discovery and clinical development phases. In other words, they don't yet have commercial products. As they prepare to launch their first commercial product, their strategic plan needs to include developing a reliable sales force. Since this core competency is vital to its success, top-level management should develop the strategic initiatives necessary to realize it. The strategic planning could result in several possible ways to satisfy the core competency requirement:

- Outsource all sales activities to a non-competitor.
- Hire an experienced sales executive to build a new sales organization.
- Acquire a small company that has a commercial sales force.
- Merge with another company to achieve sales and other synergies.

Discussions of strategic goals, strategic initiatives, critical success factors, and core competencies can be long and intense. If the participants are well grounded in the rules of engagement and background filters, and if the visioning session is conducted in a way that allows new ideas to flow freely from each individual, such discussions will be meaningful, productive, and exciting.

Every time I have used this method of visioning, I have gone around the room afterward and asked the participants to describe their experience in the workshop. Inevitably, I receive comments like these:

- "I've never before been able to express myself in this way in our organization."
- "I never realized the power of having a few moments of quiet time."
- "I never thought that my organization was capable of such creativity."
- "I've never felt a deeper sense of connection with my peers."
- "I've never seen so many great ideas become organized in such a short period."
- "I never thought we'd finish with so many people at the session, but we did."
- "I never thought my people were capable of generating such innovative ideas."
- "I never would have believed what we were capable of achieving in two days."

The list goes on and on.

The results of a visioning session can seem almost miraculous, but when you think about it, the reasons for success are pretty simple. The grounding information provides a solid foundation for the visioning as well as some real insights into what the issues and opportunities are. Next, the guided visioning helps screen out mind chatter, allowing participants to empty their minds so new ideas can emerge from a place much different than the rational brain. Then comes the show-and-tell. As each participant's ideas are discussed and leveraged, the participants are further aligned with one another, and even more creative new ideas flow from the original ideas that emerged during the visioning retreat. Finally, all the new ideas are organized in a way that is simple to understand, concise, and easily communicated.

Nearly all who have experienced this process agree that the visioning exercise is truly transformative. It connects all of them via a higher, egoless state, to innovative ideas based on a common vision and fosters positive and lasting changes among the participants and their organization. At the end of these sessions, participants actually *feel* as if they have already achieved success, because of the techniques used in the visioning process. Having actually *felt* the success during their vision, they now *know* that it can be achieved again, in the real world.

Executing the steps outlined in this chapter will require both a personal and collective commitment not to return to the old ways of incrementalism and mediocrity. If you try to turn back to the ways of old after launching into the fifth ring, your entire organization will lose its faith, along with the belief that true excellence can ever be achieved.

Ensuring that there will be no turning back is as easy as 1-2-3:

1. Allow visionary ideas to emerge at all levels.
2. Establish and hold a collective intention.
3. Foster an attitude of positive, can-do thinking.

Keep these important principles for success in mind as you continue reading, and remember—there can be no return.

Chapter 9

# Assessing the Impacts of Planned Change

IN THE BOOK OF Emptiness, Musashi makes the following statement: "Consciousness and external reality are both real only in relation to each other. Or to put it another way, all that exists, exists only in relation to other things.... It is the relationship that counts, not the *things* that relate. This relationship is what Musashi calls *ku*."

In a strategic context, relationships are critical because of the depth and breadth of their impact. Therefore, you'll need some way to assess each strategic initiative in relation to the others to determine the effort it will require to implement it, as well as the value it will bring to your organization. If executed properly, such an evaluation will provide you with a simple, yet holistic means of prioritizing your strategic initiatives with regard to sequence of implementation and resource allocation. Assessing your strategies is the next important step in the Fifth Ring Strategy.

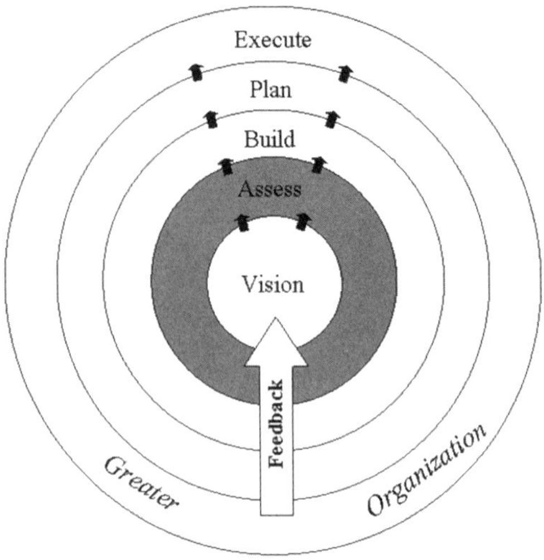


Figure 22. Assessing the Strategies of the Fifth Ring

## Determining the Criteria

The first task of strategic assessment is to determine the criteria for the prioritization process. This will allow all participants to agree on the reasons for giving an initiative a higher or lower priority, thus minimizing subjectivity. It will also ensure that items that aren't essential to the mission won't end up at the top of the list.

### *Using a Collaborative Prioritization Chart*

The collaborative prioritization chart is a very useful tool. I have used them again and again in various forms to accomplish various objectives. Unable to determine its origins, I created my own version of it for the sole purpose of prioritizing strategic initiatives (see figure 23).

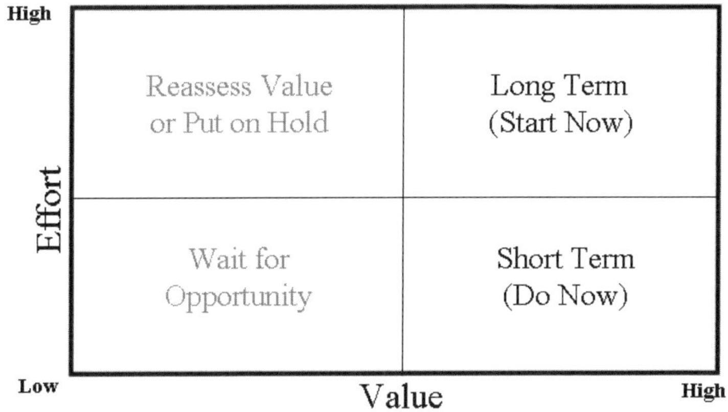


Figure 23. Collaborative Prioritization Chart

This chart, which I call the "Chopping Block," encourages thought-provoking discussion of the value and resource requirement of each initiative. Both effort and value criteria should be customized for each application in order to forge a bond of agreement among the participants with regard to the meaning of each axis.

## *Required Effort*

Effort is the total sum of the resources required to execute a given strategic initiative from beginning to end. All resources should be considered and evaluated together, holistically. The following table provides some examples of resources that are frequently considered in such an exercise.

Table 2. Sample Resource Requirements

| **Resource Type** | **Description** |
|---|---|
| Time | Time is a key resource and will often come with some cost implication in terms of supporting a strategic initiative. Limiting the allocation of time can result in lost or reduced opportunity, so time must be carefully considered. Be sure to consider external costs, such as consulting and third party vendors. |
| Money | Money is perhaps the most obvious resource requirement, as most other resources usually end up costing money. To keep things simple, some organizations limit their resource types to money and time. However, measuring money alone isn't recommended, as it's often impossible to put a cost on everything. |
| Human Capital | Human capital includes the various levels of skill needed to execute a strategic initiative. Human capital includes not only internal labor, but also external contract employees, and temps that are needed for a portion of the initiative. Skills that are hard to come by will push the resource requirement higher. |
| Intellectual Property | Intellectual property includes such items as patents, trademarks, copyrights, recipes, and even bills of material for certain manufacturing processes. These often come with a price, or must be purchased. |

| Resource Type | Description |
|---|---|
| Tools | Tools can range from large manufacturing equipment (which will ultimately end up in the money category), databases, information systems, analytical reports, methodologies, and standardized processes that can be leveraged. |
| Physical Material | Physical material can be viewed as either material the organization has that can be used for leverage, or material it will need to acquire in order to execute an initiative.<br>The latter will typically come with some cost. If it is hard to obtain, time may also need to be factored in. |
| Third-Party Alliances | Third-party alliances are the partnerships needed when an organization doesn't have the core competency or access it needs to accomplish its objective. Such alliances can be either competitive or noncompetitive, such as the classic "co-opetition" scenario in which companies with like products or services agree to collaborate in order to purchase a needed resource in bulk in order to reduce cost. |
| Volunteers | Volunteers are a crucial element in all types of nonprofit organizations. Volunteerism comes with a cost in either time or money, but the return on investment can be enormous, depending on the service. |

Prior to beginning the prioritization exercise, the participants should discuss the options for resource requirement criteria and decide which ones they want to use to evaluate each strategic initiative. These criteria should then be used as a general guideline. Although I've seen complex quantitative models used for this purpose, I would recommend avoiding too much detail. If two initiatives are close in priority and competing with each other for funding, a more detailed assessment can be done for clarification. But to do this for each one on each criteria point will defeat the purpose of doing a collective prioritization session in which the entire group intuitively determines the outcome.

*Value to the Organization*

The next axis for consideration during the prioritization exercise is the value that a given initiative has to offer the organization. Value can be perceived in various ways. Table 3 displays some examples of value-based criteria that you might consider while assessing your various strategic initiatives. Again, these criteria would be considered together, holistically, as was done in the *resource* table.

## Table 3: Sample Value Types

| Value Type | Description |
|---|---|
| Return on Investment | Return on investment should include considerations of both hard (i.e., financial) returns and soft, or intangible, returns. A formal business case is typically done prior to each new project to validate the opportunity, so ROI at this stage should be limited to the best educated guess of those participating in the prioritization exercise. |
| Contributions to Shareholder Value | Shareholder value contribution (or stakeholder value in some cases) includes the impact on all significant financial metrics and key performance indicators that are likely to positively influence shareholder value. |
| Customer Satisfaction | Customer satisfaction is the contribution a strategic initiative will likely make by contributing usefulness, helpfulness timeliness, or even fun to the customer's lifestyle through either product or service. |
| Organizational Image | Organizational image is the impact a strategic initiative will likely have on its community, region, country, and the world. By including charitable or environmental activities as a strategic initiative, many organizations have achieved amazing results by enhancing their image in the eyes of the consumer. |

| Value Type | Description |
|---|---|
| Competitive Advantage | Competitive advantage includes any advancement in the competitive realm, including overcoming barriers to entry, threats of substitution or new entrants, bargaining power of suppliers or buyers, or any other threats posed by existing or potential competitors or influencers. |

As with developing resource requirement criteria, the group should discuss and strive to agree on the final list of value types to be used during the prioritization of strategic initiatives. Adding too much complexity and analysis at this stage will detract from a holistic evaluation of each initiative relative to the others. If there's still disagreement after the prioritization exercise, a detailed business case analysis can be performed to determine which of any competing initiatives will take precedence.

### *Conducting the Prioritization Exercise*

The prioritization exercise will normally take place toward the end of the strategic visioning retreat, while representatives from the entire system are still assembled in one place. Occasionally, time limitations will preclude this from happening at the same retreat, in which case the leadership team should plan another half-day meeting for the prioritization.

When I'm preparing to facilitate a prioritization exercise, I create a large replica of the collaborative prioritization chart, or chopping Block (see figure 23) and post it in the front of the room where all participants can see it. Next, I write each revised strategic initiative on an individual sticky note and put the notes in the front of the room next to the chart. I then explain the process to the group and answer any questions before beginning the exercise.

The exercise begins when I select the sticky note with the first strategic initiative and ask the group what it would take to execute it (i.e., effort), given the criteria they agreed upon before the exercise. The sticky note will shift from the bottom to the top along the center vertical line until the group has come to an agreement on the position. Agreement will be reached only after in-depth discussion to clarify perceptions of why the resource requirement should be higher or lower.

Next, using the same initiative, I ask the group to assess the value it would most likely bring to the organization. As they discuss value, the initiative will travel from left to right on the chart until it lands on an agreed-upon position along the horizontal axis.

The first initiative will always be the most difficult to position, as there's no context of relationship between it and the resource requirements of other initiatives. As other initiatives are added to the chart, however, they take on new meaning when viewed in relationship with the others. Then some of the previously posted initiatives will likely be repositioned. Even after the last initiative is posted, the discussion should continue to ensure that the group has agreed upon the final resting point of each initiative.

Each quadrant in which an initiative lands will have a different meaning as it relates to the timing and effort of execution. If an initiative lands in the lower right quadrant (high value, low cost), it's considered ripe, low-hanging fruit. Such initiatives should be executed as soon as possible in order to create credibility and momentum behind the strategic planning and management process. If an organization is able to see immediate results from the planning session, it will be more likely to buy into the process, deem it a success, and get on board with the changes yet to come.

The upper right quadrant represents high-value initiatives that will be more costly from a resource perspective. You shouldn't shy away from these initiatives just because of the resource requirements. Instead, you should consider breaking them down into achievable tasks that will withstand the pressures of scrutiny and demonstrate continuous success until the ultimate completion of the initiative. Higher-cost, higher-effort initiatives can quickly lose momentum if success isn't demonstrated soon after their inception.

The lower left quadrant displays those initiatives that are of lower value, yet not very difficult to achieve. These should be set aside until the right opportunity arises, such as in conjunction with a complementary initiative for which the necessary resources will already be committed.

The upper left quadrant represents initiatives that are too high in resource cost given the value they are likely to bring at this point in time. Initiatives that end up in this quadrant should either be put on hold until the initiatives with higher value are completed, or closely evaluated to ensure that no attempt is being made to advance a low-value idea, or even a personal agenda – hence the word "chopping block."

Figure 24 shows an example of a completed prioritization chart that would have been done for a large Fortune 500 consumer products company. In this case, participants initially believed that all initiatives would end up in the right two quadrants. However, as discussions continued and the participants began to see the deeper meaning and value of each initiative in relationship to the others, they began to realize that some things should take precedence over others, for reasons of both value and effort. Slowly some initiatives began to move into the left two quadrants.

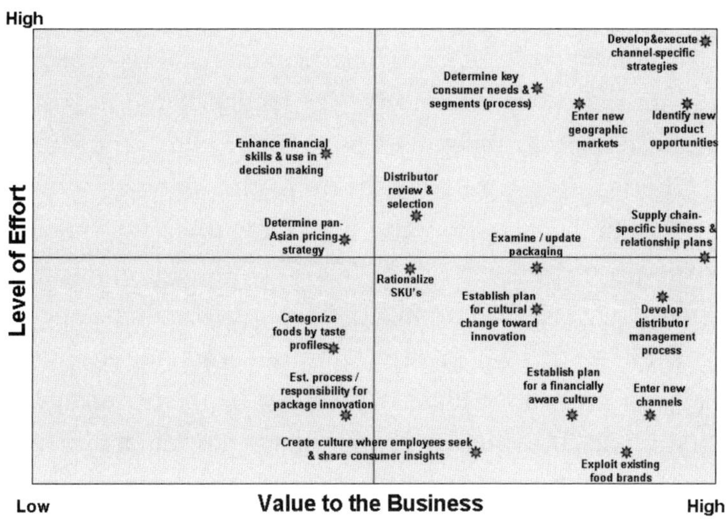


Figure 24. Sample Prioritization Chart

Trying to read each of the dots as an outsider, you might find little or no meaning in any of them. However, I can assure you that every one of the participants in the prioritization session fully understood each initiative, its value, its required effort, and its relationship to each of the others after the exercise was done.

One way to ensure that strategic initiatives are being evaluated based on their true merit is to reintroduce the double-loop learning process. As each initiative is being discussed, there will likely be some different opinions about either value or resource requirement. I encourage those holding strong opinions to elaborate their position and then allow the other participants to provide feedback of their own views on the subject. This not only exposes any hidden personal agendas, but also serves as a great learning and alignment opportunity for all participants. This is especially true for those asked to receive the feedback and introspect on those feelings they attached to their original position.

The facilitator must be aware of the balance between wisdom and innovation and how they affect the outcome of the prioritization process. Those who have much more experience and wisdom in a certain area should be encouraged to use it in a positive manner and not merely to discredit innovative ideas that cannot be measured against experience. If someone claims that a particular initiative has been attempted before and failed, the group shouldn't take the comment as a sign of defeat. Rather, they should discuss the past experience. This will allow ideas to emerge that might provide a different, more successful means of achieving it.

Innovative ideas should be challenged by wisdom and experience, but never discounted. Achieving a healthy balance between wisdom and innovation can keep an organization from losing the vision generated earlier in the session and reduce skepticism through collaboration and the sharing of progressive new ideas.

## Developing a Strategic Roadmap

When all of the strategic initiatives have been put into perspective via the prioritization process and it has been determined which ones will be executed immediately, the group should begin to develop a high-level strategic roadmap. This will put the relationships of strategic initiatives and milestones into perspective by showing each initiative in relation to the others along a time horizon.

The roadmap should be developed on a single page so that relationship isn't sacrificed for detail. Figure 25 depicts a roadmap used by a medical device subsidiary of a life sciences company that was preparing to launch its new strategic initiatives. The roadmap shows the required steps involved in ramping up the organization so it could to meet its product launch milestone at the end of 2006, the anticipated FDA approval date of its new product.

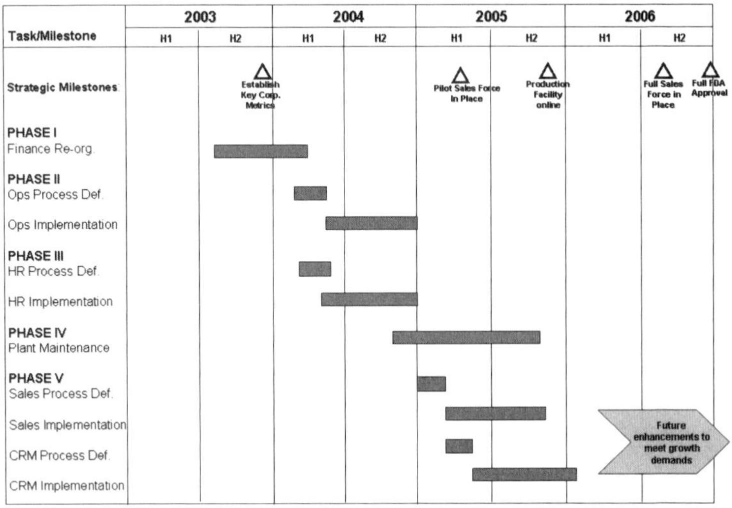


Figure 25. Sample Strategic Roadmap

The plan starts with the triangular milestones across the top of the plan. These milestones are what drive the key activities, or strategic initiatives, which are represented by the blue lines. The lines show the anticipated duration of each task in relation to the calendar across the top of the plan (H1 and H2 represent first and second half of a given year).

The idea here is not to generate mountains of documentation. The plan should simply show the relationship of each task to the others that are required to successfully launch the new product. It can also show the critical path, or the order in which each initiative will have to be executed in relation to the others.

Because such a plan requires some extended contemplation and perhaps deeper analysis, it might not be completed during a two- to three-day strategic visioning retreat. The participants can, however, discuss the next step: lining up the right people to develop a high-level roadmap. This simple, yet effective representation of the strategic initiatives will provide the perspective necessary for the next level of planning, which will be done by the teams chosen to implement the new vision.

## Conducting Follow-Up Assessments

You should go through the prioritization process at least once a year, even though a visioning retreat might not precede it. The prioritization exercise should begin exactly where it left off the last time. Your executive team should review each initiative, discuss its status in detail, and remove any that have been completed since the last review from the chart. They might wish to revisit those that were put on hold because of limited funding or other resource constraints. They should then discuss the remaining initiatives both individually and collectively to determine if their priorities have shifted in one direction or the other. Finally, they should decide whether they should begin executing these tasks given the resources currently available, or whether they should remove some from the chart altogether.

As time passes, priorities often tend to shift. Some initiatives may not carry the same weight they did during the initial planning session. Your executive team should examine such initiatives closely to see whether or not it makes sense to continue with plans to fund them. The team should be open and honest during such an assessment and not be afraid to ask the tough question—whether to move forward with the original idea, or scrap it all together.

By reviewing each initiative on a periodic basis, you can avoid the classic Abilene Paradox, where an organization gets on a path nobody wishes to go down, but the individual members of the organization believe that they are the only ones who don't want to take that path, so they remain quiet. More importantly, such periodic reviews will help you avoid major costs that are no longer likely to bring value without any one person losing credibility or feeling as if he or she has failed. Such decisions are made by joint executive decision and are based only upon objective value.

Periodic follow-up assessments like these are an opportunity for the executive team to come together for realignment and reflect on the progress that has been made toward achieving each of the strategic goals, and the changes that may have occurred in the market. Many executives are surprised and excited to see all that has been done since the previous planning session, especially if they are used to working in an organization that hasn't previously utilized the integrated planning process of the Fifth Ring Strategy. Witnessing such progress can motivate and reinvigorate your executives.

I recall working with a large international industrial manufacturing company. Like many companies, they originally called me in to turn around a failed strategic initiative. It had gotten out of control and cost the company tens of millions of dollars, with no end in sight. I took the executive team through a strategic visioning session to realign the company starting at the top, as this is where most of their problems had originated due to lack of executive sponsorship, vision, and alignment.

Eight months later, after many of the issues had been resolved, I was still working with them on various strategic initiatives, and we decided that a follow-up review was necessary to reprioritize the initiatives that hadn't yet been executed. As the review was taking place, the executives were totally astonished to discover the progress that had taken place since the turnaround efforts began. This turned them into true believers. They began to make more aggressive and innovative plans, knowing that their organization was capable of accomplishing them.

If we truly expect our customers, suppliers, competitors, and even the markets in which we operate to change, and change frequently, why shouldn't we expect our strategic plans to change as well? Better yet, why can't we be the driver of change? This is at the heart of what complexity theory teaches us, yet we continue to create five-year plans that we expect to carry our organization through the next half-decade. Worse yet, we believe that we can predict what the future will look like several years out, without planning for adjustments. We are only fooling ourselves.

Although I realize that most shareholders, banks, and large customers demand documented three-to five-year plans, this doesn't mean that you have to wait three to five years to revisit them. If you can make strategic planning and management an ongoing meta-process in your organization, you'll have no need for a plan that you revisit and renew every five years. Your organization will be more fluid, and your executives' sights will be aligned and set on the horizon. They will be continuously generating new visionary ideas and moving your organization toward positive change and prosperity in real time.

# Chapter 10

# Building Cross-Functional Teams

THROUGHOUT *THE BOOK OF Five Rings*, Musashi says that you need to master the techniques of all schools if you want to be able to operate in the state of enlightenment without distraction. While you're building the teams needed to execute your organization's strategic plans, you want to be certain that you don't have to figure everything out as you go. You want to make sure that the right people with the right knowledge are in place, working together, and paving the way for effective strategic change.

Therefore, building the proper teams for strategic execution is the next important link in the chain of success. This chapter will provide you with the knowledge you need to make sure you're choosing the right people and building the right teams for strategic execution.

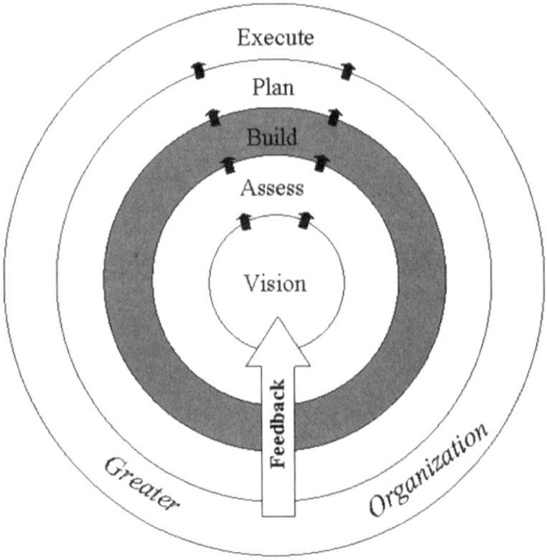


Figure 26. Building the Teams of the Fifth Ring Strategy

## Teams 101: Understanding the Basics

Team-based dynamics can contribute greatly to both individual and collective strategic success. Teams can be highly effective at all levels of the organization, and development can be achieved within every team.

A team (as opposed to a group) consists of individuals who share a common vision or set of goals. Since the members have common goals to attain and a limited amount of time to complete their tasks, they will typically operate in a consensus-based mode. If a team is operating effectively, there will also be a high degree of synergy that expedites learning for all the individuals involved. A team made up of people with diverse, yet complementary, backgrounds and skill sets will achieve a high level of performance.

To provide a bit more insight into team dynamics, let's look at the five levels of teams that Jon Katzenbach and Douglas Smith describe in their book, *The Wisdom of Teams*.

1. A *common working group* is the normal group of individuals in a department who work together but have individual goals and objectives. The only performance needs or opportunities are those at the individual level.
2. A *pseudoteam* isn't yet focused on or trying to achieve collective performance, although the potential is there. The need for a common vision is present, but the individuals are working on their own objectives.
3. A *potential team* has a significant performance need and is trying to increase its impact on the organization but hasn't achieved any greater impact than the common working group.
4. A *real team*, which consists of members with complementary skill sets, is committed to a common purpose, need, and approach. This synchronized, harmonious working dynamic pushes its performance impact to a higher level than normal.
5. A *high-performance team* has all the attributes of a real team. However, each individual on the team is also committed to the growth and success of all other team members. A high-performance team attains a much higher level of performance and effectiveness than the others.

Clearly, you want your teams to be in the high-performance category. When they reach this stage, they will be characterized by:

- Constructive conflict
- Risk taking
- Helpful criticism
- Objectivity
- Active listening
- Mutual support
- Recognition

A team consisting of members who actively monitor each other's skill sets and capabilities becomes a self-correcting, or cybernetic, system that helps develop all team members so they can achieve the overarching strategic objectives. High-performance team dynamics also promote a healthy level of tolerance for failure, as opposed to the insecurity and paralyzing fear that an individual nonteam member typically experiences. Furthermore, ego-driven individualism (this is not meant in a derogatory sense) becomes a self-monitoring mechanism. Peer pressure will quickly correct individuals who behave in an egotistical manner because their behavior prevents the entire team from meeting its common objectives

Now that we have seen what an effective team looks like, let's expand this concept to another realm. When we observe the various levels of team dynamics in an organization, we begin to see the effectiveness of not just the team itself, but also of inter-team dynamics. In other words, we see how well teams work with each other at various levels in the organization.

Referring back to the embedded alignment cycle discussed in Chapter 7 and the legitimate and shadow systems discussed in Chapter 2, we can see how the executive level and the implementation team level can be brought together in a highly effective interteam model.

As you recall, in figure 15 (Chapter 7) we saw the two levels of teams in any given organizational setting—the strategic (executive team) and the operational (implementation team) cycles. The executive cycle provides the organizational vision, structure, and boundaries in which the rest of the organization (i.e., the operational level) can operate. It does this through a continuous cycle of planning, introspection, and execution.

The operational cycle is prone to changes in the organization's environment and so needs to change and evolve continuously. As you'll recall, this is vital to the adaptability and ultimate survival of the organization. However, as the operational cycle attempts to adapt to the changes, it pushes against the boundaries imposed by the strategic cycle.

The tension generated at the operational level will either influence the executive level to adapt and create new parameters, or the executive level will force the operational level to conform to existing parameters. On the one hand, the executive level must establish clear tolerance criteria so that the entire system won't fall into chaos as a result of ambiguity. On the other hand, it must give in to those tensions created out of the need to maintain the vision in a changing environment.

With an interteam dynamic like this, both the executive level and the operational level influence each other and continue to learn from each other. This exchange results in collective development, provided the team dynamics at both levels are operating under the high-performance team criteria.

In a high-performance team, the members always have an introspective routine that allows the individuals in the group to rapidly and effectively develop higher levels of awareness and competency. As such teams interact they foster the development of the collective organization. This is the true essence of and the pragmatic means of becoming a learning organization.

By now, we have seen how principles of social ecology—manifested in the form of interactive teams—contribute greatly to both individual and organizational development. We have also seen how team interaction can promote the same type of growth through the principles of creative tension found in complexity theory. And finally, we have seen how we can develop and promote a sustainable learning/teaching organization through human interaction at all levels. Such an organization will continue to operate successfully in the absence charismatic leadership.

With all of these principles in place, your organization will become a complex cybernetic system that remains self-sustaining through continuous growth and change.

## Building the Right Team for Success

Now that we have a better understanding of the basics of high-performance team dynamics, let's discuss the practical guidelines for building such teams. In other words, let's see how to get the right people in the right teams and get them to do the things that will successfully implement your strategies.

Some of the most innovative ideas that come out of the strategic visioning process don't necessarily reflect the way the organization is set up to run its day-to-day business. In fact, many of these new ideas require a unique combination of skill sets working together to turn these ideas into effective solutions. If we revisit the value ring discussed in Chapter 7 (figure 17) we can begin to see how the core development teams at the center of the model can effectively implement new crossfunctional strategies.

To generate new ideas about how to achieve these new strategies, key personnel are pulled from various areas of the value ring (or chain), as well as from support areas like information services, finance, and human resources. Additionally, suppliers, third-party partners, and even customers can be pulled into the teams to provide their unique perspective. The program management office will assign some to specific projects, while others will operate on their own. But all will work toward the common vision set by the executive visioning team.

In choosing team members, you should consider several factors in addition to the skill sets. First of all, you should try to assign your best and brightest people to the teams. You may be reluctant to remove such individuals from their daily jobs because your organization depends so much on them. However, given the importance of building your organization's new strategies, you should do everything possible to pull them into the team.

These are the individuals who see their areas of responsibility as a system attached to a greater whole. Such holistic awareness is required, as they will be making decisions that will ripple throughout the entire organization. Team members need to understand the direct effects of these ripples on different parts of the organization so they can identify secondary change requirements and anticipate potential pockets of resistance. They will need to be able to access a broader group of people throughout the enterprise and to quickly assimilate their requirements and new ideas into the overall plan to ensure that all of your organization's requirements are accounted for.

The next type of individuals you should consider for the strategic team are those who are outspoken about their interest in and concern about the future of the company. You can be almost certain that such individuals will enter the project with a great deal of interest, passion, and commitment. Often they will have more commitment than other individuals who are selected to participate but hesitate to join the team because they don't want to give up their daily responsibility and the status that comes with it. Passion and commitment can sometimes outweigh a higher degree of competence or skill, provided the person chosen has an adequate skill level to start with.

The power of *commitment* has never been described better than in this loosely translated excerpt of Goethe's Faust:

> *Until one is committed, there is hesitancy, the chance to draw back, always ineffectiveness, concerning all acts of initiative and creation. There is one elementary truth the ignorance*

> *of which kills countless ideas and splendid plans: That the moment one definitely commits oneself, then providence moves too. All sorts of things occur to help one that would never otherwise have occurred. A whole stream of events issues from the decision, raising in one's favor all manner of unforeseen incidents and meetings and material assistance which no man could have dreamed would have come his way. Whatever you can do or dream you can, begin it. Boldness has genius, power, and magic in it. Begin it now.*

## A Case in Point

I once consulted a large manufacturing company that produced water purification systems for international hotel complexes and office campuses. One of the executives who approached me complained that they were having difficulty executing their strategic plan. Several strategic initiatives were costing the company millions of dollars more than planned but were producing no tangible results.

After interviewing various people at both the executive and operational levels, I quickly recognized a systemic problem that later proved to be the root of all of their problems. The executive body and the teams working on the costly strategic projects were completely misaligned. After the executive team had mandated the original projects and assembled the teams to implement the changes, they had provided no further direction or sponsorship. They quickly fell out of alignment with the project teams, which were struggling to understand what the executive team expected from them.

During these simultaneous projects, the only feedback the team ever received from the executives was when something went wrong. The only recognition any team members received was when they would jump in to fix the problem. This scenario was repeating itself more and more frequently. As it turned out, these team members were not only given no guidance for their project, but they were also not empowered to make decisions. Both team members and executives were afraid to make any decisions because of the CEO, who had built the company from the ground up, and believed that he was in total control.

The CEO was a very likeable man, but he felt compelled to call all of the shots, approve all expenditures, and determine what was right and what was wrong. Although his company was now worth five hundred million dollars, he was unable to let go of the day-to-day issues. Instead, he managed it just as he had when it was a small startup.

Every time team members took the initiative to do something, he would yell that they didn't understand the business and openly criticize what they had attempted. It didn't take long into this major strategic undertaking for them to realize that this wasn't working. But since everyone in the company was afraid to approach the CEO about the problem, they would just allow problems to occur and then try to be the first to correct them.

This pattern of behavior is what I call "heroism." It was the direct result of the CEO's control issues, which led to fear and inaction on the part of the executives who reported to him. This in turn trickled down to the project team, which received no guidance yet tried its very best to please. In their attempt to please, they ultimately turned to the dysfunctional act of heroism in order to receive status and recognition. Although this company was full of competent and highly trained people, no part of the organization reaped any of the benefits originally intended.

I knew that if the CEO of this company were willing to relinquish the tight control he held over the entire company, several things could take place to save the project:

- Executives could align themselves with a common vision.
- Executives could pass this vision on to the teams and provide ongoing guidance and direction.
- The team could have a better understanding of the directive, generate the desired results, and communicate ongoing status and feedback information to the executives.
- The executive and operational teams could work interactively as high-performance teams, driving toward the overall success of the project.
- Both executive and operational teams could be appropriately rewarded for devising proactive, well-designed strategic solutions.
- Executives and operational teams could be committed to their goals and approach them with passion and vigor.

When the interview process was over, I approached the CEO with a list of my issues and concerns, as well as the tangible and intangible results of his behavior. Being a caring individual, the CEO agreed to be coached and to receive the feedback that, if heeded, would eventually put the company into a productive mode of operation. He also agreed to hold a strategic visioning retreat and guaranteed that each individual would have an equal say in the process.

After several consecutive months of CEO coaching sessions and a successful executive visioning retreat, the planning process of the Fifth Ring Strategy was well underway. During the session, the executives created a code of conduct that ensured the fair treatment of all employees. They also empowered team members to make decisions on behalf of the executive team based on proper guidance and a full understanding of the objectives. Within just a few months the project was turned around and completed, and the company was launching the new strategic initiatives that were created during the visioning retreat. Within one year the value of this company's stock rose over twofold.

While this sad situation ultimately had a happy ending, many other organizations continue to struggle with the breakdown between executive vision and team execution. Yet all of this can be avoided with proper alignment, team building, and commitment to and at all levels of execution.

## Team Incentives

When implementing large strategic initiatives, retaining key individuals is vital to the success of the project. Turnover tends to occur frequently on such projects in the following circumstances:

- Inability to give key team members help with their

daily operational tasks, resulting in longer work hours for them

- Aggressive project milestones requiring a work pace that exceeds normal operational work hours
- Pressure from organizational expectations of a higher level of team-member responsibility, in which failure isn't an option
- Uncertainty of what is in store for team members after they complete the project that essentially changed their old job function
- Lack of appreciation and recognition of all of the above

While some strategic projects (e.g. realignment of marketing channels, corporate mergers, and so on) initially require mainly executive participation, many large strategic implementation projects will require the participation of many non-executives and require that they work harder than usual under unusually high levels of stress. In order to reduce the likelihood of untimely project turnover in circumstances like these, you will need to institute one of the three following common incentive programs to recognize and motivate participants to complete their project as planned, on time and on budget.

### *Hardship Points*

A hardship-points system is usually the least expensive option to set up, but it normally requires some additional administrative support and overhead. In this incentive program, project team members accumulate points based on the number and severity of hardships they encounter during the life of the project. Hardships include work outside of normal hours, including weekends, and excessive travel that keeps team members away from their homes and families for extended periods of time.

Hardship points can be cashed in for rewards, but only after major milestones have been met. Incentive rewards can include such things as flextime (time off during slow periods or after project completion), restaurant coupons, movie passes, or even cash. To ensure fair point distribution, the project or program manager should assign points and track them by means of some kind of formal project time-tracking system.

### *Lump-Sum Bonus*

Lump-sum bonuses are accumulated throughout the lifespan of the project and paid out to individual team members after they complete the final project task. Lump-sum amounts are based on the total time a recipient has spent on the project, minus predetermined amounts set for milestones missed and key objectives not met. This kind of bonus is the easiest to administer, as it just requires tracking the total time individual team members spend on the project. Additional amounts can be allocated to those who received no help fulfilling their operational duties, thus causing them to do additional work and work longer hours.

Lump-sum amounts should be paid in addition to normal business profit-sharing allocations, and payouts should occur shortly after the successful completion of the project.

Payouts should be awarded to all team members during a public awards ceremony held in front of the entire company, division, or department (depending on size and geographical constraints) to recognize the sacrifice and contribution these individuals have made to the organization.

### *Incremental Payouts*

Incremental payouts have been proven to be the most effective means of reducing unwanted turnover in strategic projects. These payouts are predetermined amounts paid out as each major milestone is reached. If milestones aren't reached on time, the amount of payout decreases per day until it is eventually eliminated. In such cases, the timeline is readjusted until the milestone is met, and the team tries to reach the next milestone with full payout.

As with lump-sum bonuses, incremental payouts should augment an employee's normal profit-sharing bonus, and amounts should be set higher for those whose positions aren't supported, thus causing them additional work. Each payout should be made no later than one week following the met milestone. The final payout, which is normally substantially higher than the others, should be paid out only when successful completion has been demonstrated.

In addition to these three incentive programs, there are some general guidelines that can help you reduce unwanted turnover while elevating team morale:

- Let the rest of the organization know the sacrifices the team is making to promote the good of your entire organization.
- Let the team know up front that they will need

to work longer and harder, but that they will be rewarded accordingly.

- Ask each team member in front of all others to commit to the project, the hard work, and to helping one another until they successfully complete the initiative.
- Prevent rumors by assuring all team members that they will have a desirable position waiting for them after the project is completed.

## Encouraging Regular Team Visioning

Looking again at figure 15, we can see that the operational cycle (the inner circle) is identical to the executive cycle. Once the vision has been passed down to the operational teams, they go through the same three phases of introspecting, planning, and executing.

As with the executive cycle, the first phase of the operational cycle should include a visioning exercise. Team visioning exercises start off with the same objectives as the executive visioning retreat—clearing the participants' minds of noise, performing a guided visioning walkthrough, allowing radical new ideas to emerge, and discussing, filtering, and planning. The only real difference is that while the executive visioning starts at a higher level and is based on a foundation of issues and opportunities, the operational visioning begins with the charter that outlines the overarching goal and expectations of the strategic initiative. Once this foundational information has been reviewed at the operational level, visioning can commence. Team members ponder the team's charter and explore new ideas and ways of achieving the objectives of the strategic initiative.

Visioning at this level allows the teams to find ways to resolve the stated issues by unleashing the power of many more minds—minds that are more capable and experienced in activities and issues at this level. It also gives those at this level a chance to ponder new visionary options for bringing the organization closer to a peak in the fitness landscape. Regardless of the size of an organization, when everyone in it takes time to vision in this way, its power and potential become virtually limitless.

# Chapter 11

# Planning for Action

THIS CHAPTER ADDRESSES THE planning techniques you'll need to consider to turn your strategic intentions into action. It will show you how to take the strategies outlined in the strategic roadmap in Chapter 8 and convert them into plans that are detailed enough to provide the insight and guidance needed at each level, yet not so detailed that they inhibit creativity, flexibility, and the emergence of new ideas along the way.

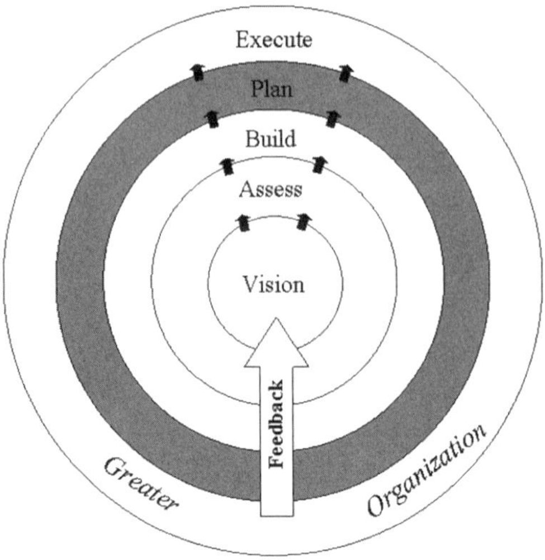


Figure 27. Planning for Action in the Fifth Ring Strategy

## Planning at the Right Level

Planning at the appropriate level for the implementation of strategic actions is crucial. Because of the high cost and high impact of such projects, proper visibility and quality control go a long way in meeting expectations and maximizing return on investment.

As they finalize the strategic plan and the strategic roadmap, executives should be aware that they probably don't have the expertise to devise the detailed requirements and design elements for any given solution. Executives often become excited about the new visionary ideas they have generated. Meaning well, they occasionally add too much detail to the plan and roadmap, even though they aren't experts in the areas affected. Not thinking about the possible ramifications of the detail they add to the plan, they pass it along to the implementation team.

When the team members look at the detailed plan, they immediately identify areas that weren't carefully thought out. Finding these solutions lacking, and knowing that they could have come up with better ones, they begin to criticize the plan and refuse to buy in to it. But, fearing the loss of their jobs or their status as part of the team, they still try to implement the plan instead of offering a better solution to the problem. They know (or at least believe) that such feedback would alienate the executive team and lose them the support they'll need throughout the project. Does this scenario sound familiar? I'm willing to bet that most of us have experienced this type of fear once or twice in our careers.

So how do you prevent this scenario from repeating itself in your organization and in your teams? Your executives must recognize their tendency to add too much detail to the strategic roadmap and intentionally hand off the high-level plan to the teams and let them plan the details. The experts chosen to carry out the work are much better equipped and much closer to the problems they have to tackle. If they weren't, the executives themselves would be (and sometimes are) on the teams.

Your executive team must also make sure it gives the members of the implementation teams clear, unambiguous and adequate information about the goal and objectives of the initiative. Too little information can lead them to misdirect funding and resources and cause them a great deal of frustration. Information regarding each strategic initiative handed over to the implementation team should include, at minimum, the following:

- Meaning of the strategic initiative and its relation to the strategic goal statement
- History and background of how the initiative came about
- Context of the initiative with regard to the current state of the organization
- Criteria that will determine the success of the strategic initiative

## Developing the Project Strategy

Once the implementation teams have received the appropriate information, they can proceed to develop and document a project strategy. The project strategy sets the boundaries for the implementation of the strategic initiative and creates a common understanding between the project teams and their sponsors before the launch of the initiative. It is a comprehensive document that incorporates all the elements needed for successful project management at all levels and is an ideal means for planning the project, articulating it, and generating consensus.

Before addressing detailed project planning considerations, it's important to understand the requirements of the project strategy. A project strategy should include, at minimum, seven components.

### *1. Project Business Case*

A project business case justifies the project at hand.

It begins with the total cost of ownership (TCO), which includes both initial costs and ongoing costs over a period of time, typically three to five years. Once the TCO is determined, each project component (such as a new feature or function) is assessed to determine the extent to which it will increase your business's capabilities.

Contribution is then broken down into hard- and soft-return categories. Hard returns are those that will have a direct and quantifiable impact on your business (for example, increased revenue and cost reduction). Soft returns are those that cannot be measured or quantified, but will nevertheless add value to your organization. Soft-return categories include customer satisfaction, employee morale, and improved corporate image, just to name a few.

The TCO is subtracted from the hard returns, and the cash differential is forecasted over a period of three to five years to show the return on investment (ROI). Soft returns are added as spice to the hard returns. Even though they may have a higher overall impact on your organization, they cannot be mixed in with the hard numbers unless they have tangible, measurable results.

### *2. Project Scope*

Project scope identifies all the areas of your organization that the project will directly impact, as well as the details of each change. Details should be in direct alignment with those outlined in the business case. Both the executive sponsors and the project teams must agree upon the project scope. You must closely manage deviations throughout the duration of the project, as they can result in cost overruns, resource shortages, and the dilution of planned results.

You can introduce a simple change-control process at the program management office level to capture each potential scope increase that will require an impact study or new business case and approval by both the project team and the executive sponsors. You need to assess the impacts of each new scope increase to ensure that time, budget, human resources, and any other related impacts are accounted for, and then readjust the project to include the new scope item. In some regulated industries such as pharmaceutical, medical device, and biotech companies, change control is mandated in certain business and support functions.

### *3. Project Team Reporting Structure*

The project strategy will normally include the structure of the implementation team and the procedures required for reporting. A team may include several subteams, which will report to a project manager, or in some instances to a program office (see Chapter 6). Team reporting requirements should be spelled out in detail in the project strategy, along with the means by which the project steering committee, which consists of its executive sponsors, will oversee and ensure the success of the project. Team charts should also be included. These will contain the names and titles of each member of the team, the program office, and the steering committee.

You should describe in detail the roles and responsibilities of each position and the service-level agreements for managerial posts. Service levels are the predetermined time-frames within which a reply or resolution is required based on an issue that a team has moved up to the program office or that the program office has moved up to the steering committee. Team descriptions with clear roles and responsibilities ensure that the team will have the full commitment of the business and support departments to supply the resources needed to successfully complete the project.

### *4. Risk Management Plan*

Prior to launching a strategic project, you need to identify all potential risks and thoroughly assess their potential impact on the success of the project. Risks on such projects typically include possible disruptions or shortcomings in the teams or their environment that could negatively impact the project's anticipated results, project ROI, the timeline, resource commitments, cost or image.

Once you identify these risks, you'll need to develop a plan describing the mitigating measures and procedures to be put in place to minimize the possibility of each risk negatively impacting the success of the project. Each risk-mitigating procedure should then be communicated to team members and to those supporting them to ensure that they are aware of the risks and actively working to prevent them from becoming real threats.

### *5. Project Milestones*

Identifying a project's critical milestones is an integral part of project strategy. Milestones should be presented as a graphical representation of a timeline and explained, milestone by milestone, in full detail. Milestones display what needs to be achieved in order to guarantee the success of the project. They help executive sponsors understand the ramifications of making or missing each milestone and provide them with a way to check in with the team.

Milestones are critical targets that must be met in order for the project to be completed on time and on budget. Therefore, they should be managed from the team-member level all the way up to the executive steering committee. If each person working on the project is tracking key milestones, the teams are more likely to achieve them.

Executive sponsors play an important role in reaching milestones, as they can remove roadblocks and provide the right information at the right time. Team members can be just as critical to the successful achievement of milestones. If all team members are aware of the timing and importance of each milestone, they can communicate any issue that might cause a delay up the project reporting structure in a timely manner. This will enable them to receive the assistance they need to complete their tasks on time.

### *6. Project Budget*

A project budget is an important element in determining the success of a strategic project. But because of the high degree of complexity and the possibility of a domino effect occurring within and around the project, it can easily spin out of control. The project budget should therefore be captured in the project strategy and managed effectively in order to track costs according to each category. Project cost categories should be closely aligned with those in the business case and should include at least the following categories:

- Internal labor costs
- Third-party labor costs (consultants, contractors, and the like)
- Purchased material costs
- Support costs
- Travel-related costs
- Rental costs (facilities, equipment, etc.)

Categories should be created in conjunction with your organization's accounting department. Some costs can be capitalized and provide tax advantages, while others cannot. By capturing and managing the right cost categories, a project can save you a significant amount of money through tax advantages.

### *7. Project Approach*

The final item in the project strategy is the project approach, or methodology. The approach should provide a high-level overview of the methodology that will be used throughout the project to ensure that the proper steps are being taken toward the proper milestones. In addition to designating the methods that will be used to achieve the core activities and milestones of the strategic initiative, the approach should also outline the key steps in the methodology that will support the achievement of the following peripheral objectives:

- Business process changes
- Organizational redesign
- Assessment work

- Communications and change management
- Technical installations and implementations
- Preproject training requirements
- Postproject training and support requirements

Your teams should strive to adopt any methodology standards that have been developed and instituted. The program management office, if one exists in your organization, should then verify the methodology to ensure standardization of the approach, the tools, and any documentation templates.

While these are important guidelines for developing an effective project strategy, several commercial methodologies and project management packages available today have built-in tools and templates that can help you significantly reduce the learning curve that normally comes with such a task. If your organization is using third-party vendors (such as software vendors and consulting firms) to implement any project activities, it's best to check with them to see if they have methodologies or sample planning documents that are specific to the work at hand and can help reduce your ramp-up time.

As depicted in figure 28, once the project strategy is completed, detailed action planning can begin, which begins with determining project success criteria.

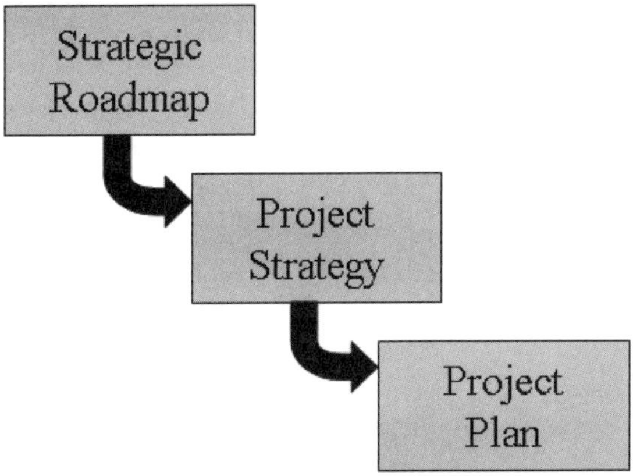


Figure 28. Strategic Project Planning Progression

## Measuring Project Success

You can significantly increase the probability of the success of a strategic project, first, by understanding its objectives and the anticipated value it will bring to your organization and, second, by translating this information into success criteria against which the project can be managed. Success criteria should be communicated to each individual involved in the project, whether directly or indirectly. Executive sponsors, process owners, part-time affiliates, consultants, and even the broader community impacted by the change should be aware of the success criteria and work to both support the team and hold the team accountable for achieving them.

All team members must thoroughly understand the success criteria and how their area of responsibility will help achieve them. There are basically two categories for success in any given strategic project. The first is simply that the objectives were achieved; the second is whether or not they were achieved on time and on budget.

The first category can be accomplished by outlining the goals and objectives of the project, the value anticipated by each goal, and the precise metrics that will determine whether that goal has been achieved. In this case, the linkages between the goal, the strategic initiatives, and the goal's success metric might look like those in figure 29.

Figure 29. Strategic Goal, Initiative, and Metrics Linkages

Using the relationship displayed in figure 29, let's assume that your goal is to improve the visibility and effectiveness of your sales force. In order to achieve this goal, you will first need to launch a strategic initiative to develop a system that collects data about unqualified leads, qualified leads, opportunities, proposals, and closings at each stage of the sales pipeline. When sales managers know which deals are at which stage in the sales pipeline, they can pinpoint the stage at which each salesperson is losing deals. With this new information and insight, your management team can intervene in the sales process to either provide a higher level of support for the salesperson, or simply to communicate where the process is breaking down.

Assuming that the actions taken on the new sales information will lower the number of lost deals, the project sponsor (for example, the vice president of sales) will need to determine the metric that must be achieved in order to be successful. While this metric is subjective, the vice president will need to solicit inputs from those who report directly to him, as well as from the CEO.

After receiving their inputs, the vice president of sales may declare that a 10 percent decrease in lost sales will need to be achieved. One of the project's key success metrics would then be the decrease of lost sales from 50 percent (current state) to 40 percent (desired state). Along with all other metrics associated with the project, the success metric is then communicated to the company and closely managed by the implementation team to ensure that they are successfully creating the means for this to happen.

The second category for success of a strategic project is whether or not a project is delivered on time and on budget. While responsibility for achieving success metrics falls to the business—in this case, the vice president of sales—on-time and on-budget delivery is the responsibility of the project team and the program management office.

Enterprise-wide strategic initiatives cost an organization an unusually large amount of money and labor to achieve. In such cases, failure isn't an option. During the early 1990s, for example, many large companies found that they needed enterprise resource planning (ERP) systems in order to maintain competitive advantage. However, when the project teams tried to implement these systems across all core business processes of their companies, many failed, either because of inexperience or lack of executive direction or sponsorship. By the time the executives realized that these projects weren't making progress, many companies had run out of money, which caused major issues with performance, shareholder value, and employee morale. The executives then had to go back to their boards to ask for more money.

While such projects were much more complex than anybody was used to back then, company executives could have avoided failure if they had been more involved in these projects and had early warning triggers that would have alerted them to the fact that a project wasn't tracking as planned. Today, there's really no excuse for such negligence. Packaged methodologies outline key milestones, and new and advanced project management tools provide visibility at various levels through advanced project management reports and scorecards, which help project managers track the progress of large initiatives. The only thing they do not provide is the discipline to follow these prescriptive guidelines.

## The Mechanics of Strategic Action Planning

Strategic initiatives differ greatly from other operational projects. Because of their higher degree of cost, impact, and risk, they require sound linkages between the strategic goal and each individual project activity and milestone. Many companies that try to implement strategies are unsuccessful mainly because of the proverbial gap between strategy and action. This gap is the result of a company's inability to put vision into action.

As you'll recall, the main purpose of developing project strategy is to translate strategic vision into a tactical and operational understanding of what it will take to carry it out. In successful organizations, the executives hand off the strategy to the operational or implementation teams, but they never actually take their hands off it. They keep their fingers on the pulse of the project to ensure that the initial strategic objectives are met. As this is happening, this same hand-off process needs to occur between the project strategy and the detailed plan.

As the project or program manager begins to link the project strategy to the detailed project plan, he begins with the elements that will turn directly into action. Figure 30 displays the four key elements required to compose a project plan that is directly linked to the strategic roadmap, and hence the strategic initiative.

Figure 30. The Four Key Elements of Planning

Project scope is the place to begin. To achieve it, you must first fully understand it, break it down into the required actionable tasks and milestones, and then arrange the tasks and milestones in an order conducive to a successful implementation. You must identify critical path items—those that must be accomplished before moving on to subsequent tasks—and arrange then accordingly.

Next, you need to review the timing of each step to determine how long it will take you to achieve each milestone. This will give you a clear understanding of how long the entire project will take and why. Once you've accounted for the timing, you'll have a better understanding of what resources you'll need to deploy at each stage of the project, as well as a bottom-up understanding of what the overall cost of the project will be. If effectively communicated, a detailed plan of this sort will show all team members the place of each task in the greater whole of the strategic initiative and allow them to manage their own tasks to completion.

If multiple consecutive projects are all working simultaneously toward a common strategic goal, you should have a program management office (PMO) in place to ensure that organization-wide standards, tools, templates, and planning techniques are being used. In most cases, members of one team will have to communicate with another team at some point, and if you standardize document formats and project planning techniques across teams, you can significantly reduce the learning curve.

It also makes sense to synchronize the project plans

and milestones of each project with the critical path activities and milestones to ensure successful achievement of the overarching goal. Such interproject coordination is the very heart of the PMO's charter. It can arrange interproject meetings and establish points of coordination to ensure that related projects interface in the right way at the right time.

## "Big-Bang" vs. Phased Approach

When deciding how to implement a strategic initiative, you should pay close attention to the phasing of the various stages. For example, if you're conducting an organization-wide business process redesign, you should consider whether or not you have all of the resources and funds needed to implement such an undertaking.

Risk is another consideration. If you put all your eggs in one basket in an attempt to achieve a high-value, high-cost strategic goal all at once—the big-bang approach— and things go wrong, you may end up with more than just a failed project. Such project failures have resulted in major losses in shareholder value, extensive lawsuits, and even bankruptcy. Hershey Foods and the Denver Airport are just two of many examples of situations where too much risk and too much money were riding on the success of a single project. Before you implement a big-bang approach, you'll want to consider the following phasing strategies:

- Resource allocation phasing
- Cash flow phasing
- Risk mitigation phasing

Many organizations—especially smaller companies that are anticipating rapid growth but don't have many resources available—consider phasing large strategic projects to make sure that an adequate number of resources will be available to accomplish each task successfully. With a high-level understanding of the vision and its objectives, you can usually phase projects to ensure proper resource coverage.

If you don't take resource coverage into consideration, major setbacks can occur throughout the project. Unanticipated resource limitations can lead to excessive consulting costs, or worse yet, to project delays and extensions. Each department supporting the project must carefully assess resource demands for each project task. Functional and support executives must commit to allocating the necessary resources and agree to support operational positions so that costly incidents don't occur.

Another reason to consider phasing a project is cash-flow limitations. When project plans carry heavy costs (usually because of such necessities as expensive equipment, facility construction, or large consulting team requirements) and you can't bear the costs because of a limited cash flow, you should consider cash flow phasing. This gives you the flexibility to implement higher-priority, higher-return functions first and lower-priority items at a later time.

You should build cash flow buffers into each project to ensure that you don't run out of money as a result of a project delay. Some organizations maximize the project scope and push their cash flow to its full capacity. If their project goes over budget, which isn't unusual, it can jeopardize the organization's financial position. While sometimes more expensive in the long run, phasing a project to meet cash flow limits will allow you to achieve your goals without the risk of breaking the bank.

The third reason to phase a strategic initiative is risk mitigation. Some strategic initiatives (such as implementing full-scale, enterprise-wide systems) add value by giving a company total visibility into all aspects of the business. As appealing as this may sound, it carries a tremendous amount of risk along with the value. When the day comes to flip the switch from the old systems, processes, or organization to the new, can you be sure that everything will work as planned, even though things have been thoroughly tested? Can you be certain that it will fulfill all it promised to the business? Are you sure that nobody will complain, or worse yet, demand that the old system be put back in place?

By phasing such projects, you have the ability to pilot certain processes in one isolated segment of the business. This allows others to assess it, demand changes, or accept what it has to offer. Pilot programs can be isolated by business unit, subsidiary, geography, or even at the department level. Furthermore, they can focus on one type of functionality (for example, sales force automation) that may run the risk of not being accepted. They can also be kept in just one part of the organization until the desirable results are achieved. Then they can then be rolled out to the rest of the organization.

Whatever the reason—resource constraints, cash flow, or risk—you can combine phasing strategies and design them to fit the unique circumstances of your organization.

While some organizations will still choose the big-bang approach for one reason or another, you should at least consider a phasing strategy, as it can bolster the probability of success.

## A Case in Point

A mid-sized biotech company once decided to implement a company-wide enterprise resource planning solution that would provide integration and visibility throughout key areas of the business, including finance, purchasing, sales, operations, and human resources. This project would cost more than $20 million US dollars, which was a lot of money for a company this size. Outside of the company's research and development pipeline, the project was the most important internal strategic initiative the company had undertaken in years. Because of the size of the organization and the risk of attempting to implement all areas at once, the company decided to phase the implementation in the following manner:

- Phase 1: Finance and purchasing
- Phase 2: Operations and human resources
- Phase 3: Sales and other enhanced functionalities

When the company implemented the first phase of the project, they had trouble getting the internal resources they needed to accomplish the necessary tasks. They had to bring in more and more consultants to compensate for the shortages. As a result, they paid much more than anticipated. The project was also delayed for several months, which nearly cost the organization more than it could afford at the time. Needless to say, at all levels of the organization there were a lot of very embarrassed people asking both for forgiveness and much more money.

When the company planned the second phase, instead of planning appropriately and requiring the full commitment of team resources, they took another tack. They planned the project at an extremely detailed level, laying out all the necessary tasks and assigning each person to each task on nearly an hourly basis. After the plan was developed, the project manager, along with the business process owners, identified the individuals who would work on the project. When those people started working on the team, they were surprised to see not only the level of detail in the plan, but also the sequence in which the tasks were ordered. They had no flexibility and little say in how the tasks should be executed, as they weren't involved in the scoping or planning activities.

During the project, people became more and more apathetic about its success. Some team members indicated that they felt like factory workers. Attitudes were at an all-time low for team members, and their negativity slowly spread to the rest of the company. The targeted users of the new processes began to anticipate the worst possible outcome, rumors began to emerge from all parts of the company, and fear snowballed.

This story would have had a much worse ending if the company hadn't decided to assess the situation and design an intervention program that would bring the project back on track. After realizing what had happened, the executive team pushed out the project timeline to allow the implementation team to reassess the plans and make changes that would be more appropriate for the business areas they represented and for the company.

The team quickly presented change requests to the executive team, and they were able to demonstrate the value of each change with a short business case. When the project resumed its course, the company created a change-management position in the project team (which they originally deemed unnecessary) and made it responsible for establishing communications between the team and the targeted users. End users were brought in to view the new design plans, and each department ended up receiving the functionality it wanted and needed. The project was ultimately deemed a success, even though it was delayed for several months in each phase, and there were additional costs.

This situation could have been avoided by taking into consideration these simple precautionary measures:

- Take time to ensure that the project team fully understands the requirements and allow them to create the detailed requirements.
- Avoid planning at a level of detail that prevents flexibility of execution.
- Avoid having only outside consultants identify the business requirements.
- Institute change management early on and ensure that the user community previews the future state.
- Ensure that early warning mechanisms are in place to trigger a prompt response when incidents threaten to disrupt the progress of a project or

generate unwarranted fear and negativity about the anticipated results.

Once you've thoroughly planned how to turn your strategy into action, you'll be ready to launch your strategic initiative and lead ongoing strategic change. In the final chapter, we'll bridge the gap between strategic planning and strategic management.

This integrated process isn't just a linear sequence of events, but rather a continuously cycling process flow that will engage all levels and resources of your organization. Fifth Ring Strategy allows your organization to act as one integrated and unified organism with the perpetual goal of continuous self-preservation, self-discovery, self-improvement, and self-renewal—all driven by a common set of intentions that sit firmly upon a foundation of forward-thinking vision.

# Chapter 12

# Launching and Leading Strategic Change

EVERY SPONSOR AND EVERY stakeholder of a strategic project or program should strive to understand the elements that differentiate strategic project management from project management on a much smaller scale. Strategic projects and programs often require the engagement of many people across different areas of the organization. This creates a monumental degree of change for the organization, which if not understood, can result in cost overruns, missed deadlines, missed opportunities, and total project, or even organization-wide failures. Projects that have so much influence on the future performance of your organization, and which can potentially cost millions of dollars to implement, deserve a much higher level of attention and ownership.

Executing, or launching and leading a strategic initiative, is the stage at which strategic goals are realized and beneficial change comes to the entire organization. While logic tells us that this is a good thing, experience warns us that during the execution of such initiatives, there are many traps and pitfalls that can render a strategy completely impotent. Even if you have the most beneficial strategic solutions, if you don't properly introduce them to the members of your organization, they may be reluctant to accept the change and eventually doom it to failure.

To prevent this from happening, you can apply four principles to each strategic change initiative while you execute it:

- Kick off the strategic initiative.
- Maintain project momentum.
- Avoid the valley of despair. (see figure 33)
- Provide for unceasing direction, feedback, and learning.

These principles will minimize the risk of perceived failure and maximize your chances to successfully transition the strategic solutions to the greater organization.

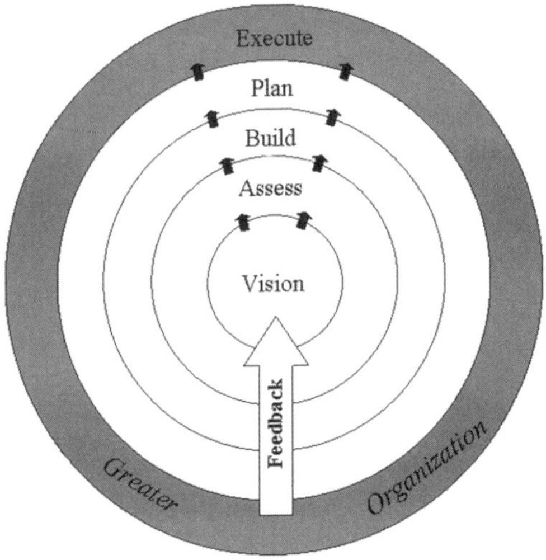


Figure 31. Executing the Fifth Ring Strategy

## Kicking Off the Strategic Initiative

After assembling your team and developing your plans, you need to launch your strategic initiative by holding a kickoff meeting. This is your opportunity to gather all your project teams, including extended project team members, and get them in alignment with the vision, the plan, and the approach.

Depending on the complexity of the project at hand, kickoff meetings can last anywhere from one or two hours to several days. Shorter meetings can be held for teams that have already worked together on preceding phases of the same project. In this case, the meeting is to briefly review the strategic vision and then provide the updates that pertain specifically to the new phase. Longer meetings are typically held in cases where a new project is beginning with an entirely new team. In cases where a strategic approach requires each team member to have an in-depth knowledge of each execution step, some training might be necessary.

Whether a kickoff meeting lasts a couple of hours or days, and however much education needs to take place, it should meet six basic requirements.

### *1. Include Words from the Executive Sponsors*

At the very start of the kickoff session, the executive sponsors should communicate the project vision and directives as they were discussed during the executive visioning retreat. Executive sponsors should express the vision with the same level of enthusiasm and optimism they had when they first created it. They should give the complete background of the vision, as well as the *essence* of what is expected as a result of the project. By essence, I mean the right level of detail—one that provides enough information but not so much that it keeps creative solutions from emerging from the teams later.

If there are any related initiatives that will have to be coordinated, these should also be communicated so that the teams understand the greater vision. While communicating the vision, the executive sponsors should also express their commitment to the teams and state their intent to work on their behalf by providing them with the right resources and information and removing obstacles from their path. By communicating their commitment, executive sponsors demonstrate to the teams that they aren't alone and that they will receive all the support they need to implement the initiative successfully. Hearing from the executive sponsors will reduce or eliminate fear and allow the teams to channel positive energy into the productive activities that will ultimately make the initiative a success.

### *2. Communicate the Plan and Approach*

When the executive sponsors have finished their motivational talks, the project or program manager should explain the project plan and the overall approach to be used throughout the project. The plan, along with each of the critical milestones, should be thoroughly explained to ensure that all team members understand their respective targets and the importance of each one in the overall scheme of the project. The project approach should be explained in conjunction with the plan so that team members understand how and why certain tasks need to be executed in the given order and how each task serves as a foundation for the next one along the critical path.

In some cases the project approach will necessitate in-depth training, especially when team members will be conducting workshops and facilitating planning sessions. In such cases, having a standardized way to conduct them will ensure that the same kind of information is gathered in each session, even though different team members might be acting as facilitators.

### 3. Communicate the Success Criteria

The criteria by which the project can be deemed a success should be made clear to the teams during the kickoff session. Each team member must have a through understanding of these criteria, as well as their own role in achieving them. Team members will then be able to use their knowledge, expertise, and experience to seek out creative ways to meet the criteria.

The discussion shouldn't include any suggestions or recommendations about how the teams should meet the success criteria, for this could inhibit their creativity. If you've chosen the right people for the teams, their creativity will be unleashed as they pursue the best way to accomplish the objective. If executives make prescriptive recommendations, the teams will likely strive to please them by doing what they suggest. If this happens, the optimal solution may never emerge.

### 4. Explain the Risks

An important part of every kickoff meeting—one that is unfortunately often left out—is explaining the project risks. Project risks vary immensely. They can include everything from technical uncertainties to potential resistance to change, process ambiguity, or poor historical vendor performance. Project risks should have already been documented as part of the project strategy, and they should now be discussed in detail with the team members so that they develop a thorough understanding of each one that pertains to their specific area of responsibility.

By communicating risks as such, the project manager or team leader is actually reducing the threat that a risk will impact the project. The more people are aware of a risk, the more likely they'll be to monitor and avoid it, thus preventing it from becoming a real threat. Early indications of risks result in timely resolution, and with all team members working together to monitor and control risks, the more likely it is that they will recognize one before it can do any damage.

### *5. Discuss Team Reporting Requirements*

Most teams are organized around the unique needs of the project and the skills and experiences of each team member. Therefore, teams are often quite unique in their structure, and the flow of information will differ from team to team. During the kickoff meeting, the teams' reporting requirements should be explained so that there is no doubt about what needs to be reported, to whom, and how often.

Reporting and escalation procedures typically work upward through the project and program team structure to the executive sponsors. Directives and sponsorship actions such as removing roadblocks and resolving issues then need to flow back down through the project structure in a clear and coherent manner. This way, those who need the information will receive it unaltered and in a timely manner. Subteam, project management, program management, and sponsor reporting procedures should explain how these entities will convey their status to the next level of responsibility.

### *6. Do a Team-Building Exercise*

At the end of the kickoff meeting, you should conduct a team-building exercise of some sort to allow team members to bond through some sort of playful activity. Team-building activities, if well planned, break down communication barriers and make people feel comfortable communicating with their counterparts on the project team. This can be achieved either through an inter-team competition or some other exercise, such as boat racing, mountain climbing, or even white-water rafting, that encourages team members to work together to resolve the problems that arise in a prescribed situation while still having lots of fun.

Team-building exercises shouldn't cause anxiety or excessive fear for any of the team members, but they do require some type of a common challenge that can't be met without all of the participants working together as a team. You can spice up the exercise by passing out comical prizes at a mock rewards ceremony at the completion of the exercise.

## Maintaining Project Momentum

The importance of project momentum can be best described by using the metaphor of a large concrete ball— the larger and more complex the project, the bigger the concrete ball.

Picture the concrete ball sitting in a field somewhere. Your job is to roll that ball, which weighs much more than you do, to another location far away. You push on the ball, exerting all your strength to get it moving. That in itself is an exhausting task. But once you get the ball rolling, you still have lots of work to do to keep it moving, although not nearly as much as you needed just to get started. At times, you can even roll the ball with just one hand. You roll it farther and farther, but just short of your goal, you're suddenly distracted, and you leave the ball standing for a bit while you take care of some other business.

In the meantime the ball sits in the dirt, sinking deeper into the rut it's forming by its own weight. When you return, you try to start the ball rolling again, but you realize that it will require just as much strength to start it again as it did when you first started out. This time, you have much less energy in reserve, and you fail to muster the strength you need to start the ball rolling again. So you leave the ball standing and never reach your goal.

Can you see the similarities between the story of the concrete ball and a strategic project? The law of momentum can be a powerful force that can either work for you or against you. If you know how to achieve momentum and keep it going, your company will benefit. There are several basic elements you need to consider during each strategic project to make sure it doesn't sink into the proverbial rut.

### *Empowering the Team*

The first thing to consider is team empowerment. You must give the teams chosen for strategic projects the authority to make decisions on behalf of the departments to which they report during normal operations. If they cannot be empowered because they lack the right skill or don't have the proper level of authority, they aren't the right people for the team. It's one thing to empower a team member, but another to ensure they have what it takes to meet the strategic objective.

Many organizations try to avoid adding senior personnel to strategic teams, as they don't want to remove them from their daily responsibilities. Instead, they rely on people who don't have the ability to make and execute decisions. This forces them to add an additional layer of management to the project. The chances are that this level will need to be managed by yet another level. This will create a team structure that is no longer nimble and thus not ready for rapid change. Worse yet, by the time the project is completed, senior management will be so far removed from the project that they may not know what solution has been implemented until it's too late.

If you don't assign the right people to the team, you'll have to pad your timelines by building into your plan the additional time required for decision-making. This isn't the right solution in any case, as it will guarantee that the plan will have a rocky road ahead and perhaps even doom it to failure. It is therefore wise to assign the right people at the right level—people who have the authority and know-how needed to get the job done right.

### *Communicating a Sense of Continuous Urgency*

One of the best ways to maintain momentum during strategic projects is to instill a sense of urgency by never letting up on the pressure to meet the designated milestones. Incentives are one way to motivate project team members to do this, but often they aren't enough to keep up the momentum. Messages about the importance of the project and the consequences of failure need to flow continuously from the very top of your organization. It takes a carefully crafted message to instill a sense of urgency, but not panic.

You need to take care not to make these messages overtly negative, as that will make the team members fearful, and fear will eventually drain and exhaust them. Team members should feel excited, not fearful or complacent. While it's often necessary to communicate the consequences of failure, senior management can balance such messages by reminding team members that they were chosen because of their exceptional performance and skill. This bolsters their status and, along with consistent attention, creates a Pygmalion effect (i.e., a self-fulfilling prophecy) that makes them more likely to succeed.

### *Establishing Individual Accountability*

If you don't hold team members accountable for completing a strategic initiative, it becomes very easy to distribute the blame when a project fails to meet its deadlines. Therefore, you need to establish individual accountability by assigning clear milestones and deadlines to each team member. While this often requires additional planning on the part of the project or program manager, it yields high returns, for every member of the team knows that a delay in the project can be traced back to a particular individual's failure to meet a milestone.

Holding each team member accountable for achieving

certain tasks doesn't have to convey a negative message. Accountability can be used in a positive, constructive way. If one person is falling behind, the project team can draw on extra resources to help meet the deadline. Knowing that the team is focused on helping rather than blaming keeps the individual members motivated in a positive way. In fact, team members will likely monitor themselves to ensure that they aren't falling behind in their tasks.

Everyone at some point meets an unanticipated obstacle that can cause a minor delay, but if the team is proactive, it can minimize delays and reduce the risks of missed milestones and cost overruns.

### *Rewards and Celebrations*

In addition to motivating the team by using incentives (see Chapter 10), periodic team rewards and company celebrations are great momentum builders. When a team meets major milestones, holding a public celebration is a great way to demonstrate to the entire organization that the project is both successful and adding value. Such celebrations, if warranted, tend to turn nay-saying into support and resistance into buy-in. The team and its sponsors gain credibility, and the support continues to snowball with each major achievement.

Rewards and celebrations also show the project team members that they are valued for their contributions. They are your organization's way of giving something back to the teams for all of the effort they have expended. Rewarding outstanding achievement on a team is also a way to build status, in both the eyes of a recipient's teammates and of the greater organization. If coupled with a recreational event such as an arcade visit, a small trip, or even a short dinner cruise, a celebration ceremony can give team members a chance to mingle in an environment void of stress. This allows them to strengthen their relationships while having fun in an environment that isn't demanding anything from them, but just giving back.

### *Committed Project Management and Sponsorship*

In managing strategic projects, there's a big difference between involvement and commitment. Most of you have probably heard of the bacon and egg scenario that describes the chicken as involved and the pig as committed. Well, there's some similarity in the level of commitment required at all levels to see a strategic initiative through successfully.

In order for management to be fully committed, there must be some skin in the game. Management must be held just as responsible for the outcome of the initiative as the project team members. When this is the case, they will be *committed* and will do whatever is necessary to ensure the success of the project. If this isn't the case, they will likely just be *involved*. When they are faced with decisions or actions that can cause a political ripple effect, they will most likely either avoid the situation and allow the team to fend for itself, or to take a less effective approach that will make fewer waves.

Commitment to the vision requires managers to make bold decisions and create change within the organization. Avoiding commitment will produce mediocre tactical solutions that will dilute the strategic benefits of the visionary process. Boldness is a virtue in the Fifth Ring Strategy, and such boldness requires a high level of commitment to the vision.

There's a management catchphrase that has been around for decades: *management by walking around.* This concept is so simple, yet so highly effective that I find it amazing that more managers don't practice it. It entails nothing more than walking around and chatting with various team members with no agenda or forewarning. Doing this can have a significant impact on team effectiveness. Communications that are open, honest, and unscripted typically result in some amazing insights and feedback from both the strategic project teams and the greater organization.

Some executive sponsors, and even project and program managers, choose to remain in their offices rather than get out and mingle with the team on an informal basis. They rely on status reports and standard protocol of the legitimate system. Whether their excuses are shyness or the belief that they have more important things to do, they are missing out on the richness of information that can come through the informal communication channels also known as the shadow system (see Chapter 2). By walking around and engaging in informal conversations, managers often uncover issues well in advance of a status report. This gives them an opportunity to squelch problems before they get out of hand.

This method also gives management an insight into what members of the greater organization are thinking. Both negative and positive readings provide managers with the information needed to identify both the need for intervention and the successes that can be leveraged. Management by walking around allows the legitimate and shadow systems to interact in a spontaneous, unscripted manner without attempting either to reinforce or challenge the company structure.

### *Change Management and Communications*

Once your organization has made a commitment to change, change becomes inevitable. Still, you will always meet with pockets of resistance fueled by fear and anxiety. That's why you need to make change management an ongoing activity and a formal part of any strategic project or program. In fact, it is recommended that change management be an integral part of the program management office (see Chapter 6)

Change management directs and energizes the project teams while preparing the rest of the organization to accept the changes the teams are introducing. The change management specialist, or team, should work closely with the project and program managers to develop communication and intervention plans that ensure the ultimate acceptance of the strategic change.

This requires the constant monitoring of the organization and at times allowing employees to preview the teams' achievements. This will result in valuable feedback and reduce the fear and anxiety typically caused by the unknown. Throughout the project, the change management team should gradually—not radically—transfer the team's knowledge and ownership to the greater organization (see figure 32).

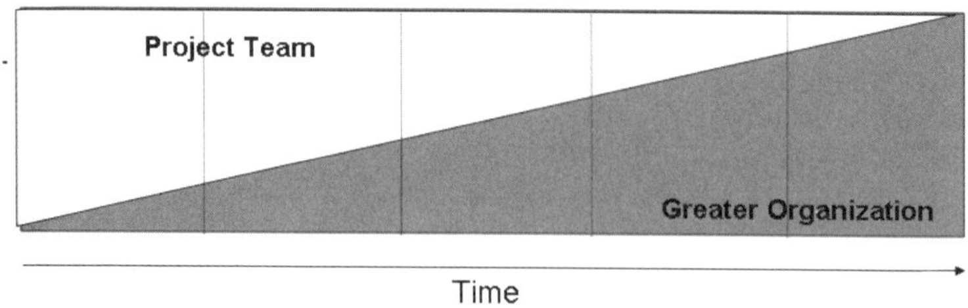


Figure 32. Uniform Transfer of Ownership

The key elements of successful strategic change include alignment, communication, and training. Although we have discussed the importance of alignment throughout this book, the change management team will need to make sure that alignment exists within a project team and with other affiliated project teams.

Additionally, and most importantly, change management must align the project initiative with the greater organization that will ultimately be the recipient of the change. This is done by means of ongoing, targeted communications between sponsors and teams and between teams and the greater organization. These communications come in various forms of media and meetings, such as:

- Targeted and organization-wide memos
- Targeted and organization-wide e-mails and voicemail messages
- Meaningful and celebratory banners and placards posted throughout the facilities
- Small lunch meetings with project teams and their targeted recipients from the greater organization

- Large company-wide, "town hall" meetings held to discuss the project's status and to allow questions

The last handoff between the project teams and the organization is training. Training must be robust enough to transfer organizational, process, and technical knowledgc to the organization. Recipients of the change must fully understand the magnitude of change upstream and downstream. They need to understand who or what will have an impact on what they will be doing and whom or what they will impact as they execute their new processes.

In many cases, training must also build at the transaction level the technical and functional skills that will allow recipients to maneuver effectively and efficiently in their new work environments. Actual work scenarios should be simulated in training sessions to show recipients how to quickly assimilate these new skills into their daily work.

As you can see, alignment, communications, and training all working together as one integrated force significantly increases receptivity to the strategic change and improves attitudes by reducing the counterproductive forces of fear and anxiety.

## Avoiding the Valley of Despair

Once a strategic initiative has been transferred to the greater organization, productivity can take a dip. No matter how much you prepare and train for them, anomalies always emerge after a project goes live. Unanticipated issues will also show up, and when they do, your company will likely slide into the proverbial valley of despair. While you can't completely avoid such anomalies, you can minimize the impact of anomalies on productivity by properly managing them.

Immediately after a project is complete (that is, when it's handed over to the greater organization), there is normally a slight increase in productivity simply because of the anticipation of an improved working environment. Then come the anomalies. They create situations that weren't planned for in different areas of the changed environment and cause disruptions in the work environment that nobody has been trained to handle. After a brief period of denial, the recipients of the new changes often fall into a period of despair (see figure 33).

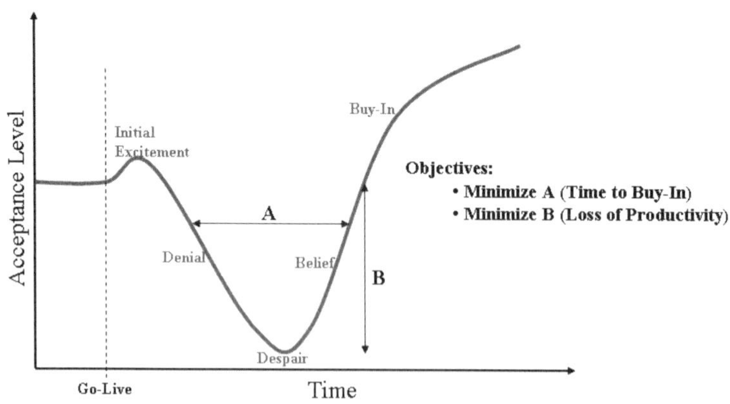


Figure 33. The "Valley of Despair"

By preparing appropriately and ensuring that knowledgeable personnel are standing by to assist those experiencing difficulties, you can significantly reduce the time your organization spends in the valley of despair. A well-organized project call center can react to the very first signs of trouble, and the lessons learned from each intervention can be posted on a project website or some other medium that the support team and the recipients can access. If the team is able to demonstrate the benefits of the new changes early on (minimize the "A" span), and keep productivity loss to a minimum (minimize the "B" span), the greater organization will be more likely to buy in to the changes, and negative perceptions will not impede productivity.

If you communicate the concept of the valley before you release the new changes to the greater organization, both the team and the recipients will understand that such setbacks, while often inevitable, are temporary. Having an early awareness of this phenomenon can motivate the team to set up the structures and procedures that will allow them to intervene at the first sign of trouble and so keep fear and anxiety at a minimum throughout the transition period.

## Practicing Continuous Direction, Feedback, and Learning

Before, during, and after implementing strategic initiatives, the entire organization must be practicing a continuous flow of direction, feedback, and organization-wide learning. This cycle must not be broken at the end of a strategic project, and members of all levels of the organization must hold each other accountable for keeping the flow of information alive.

As you'll recall in Chapter 2 I discussed the idea of cybernetics and self-organization. Continuous direction, feedback and learning are keys in developing this *flow* capability within your organization.

The flow begins when the members of the executive management team first create the new vision for the organization. As they communicate the vision to the strategic team and the rest of the organization using the tools and techniques of the Fifth Ring Strategy, they continuously receive feedback from the areas of the organization closest to the change. As they receive and process this new information, they must remain in a constant state of aligned fluctuation. As displayed in figure 34, this will enable them to pass down new directives that embody the feedback they have received.

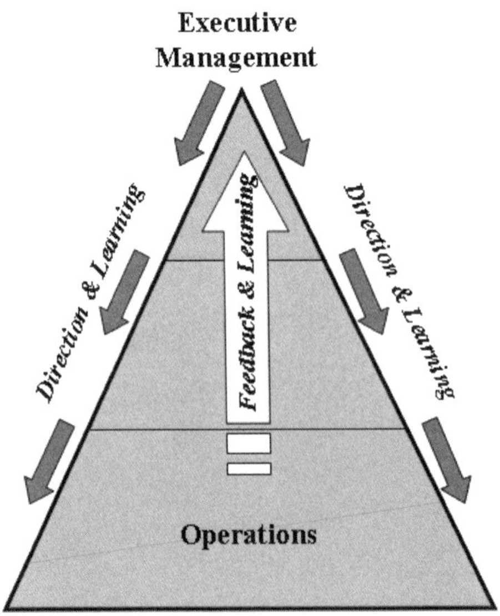


Figure 34. The Continuous Emergence Model

When the strategic initiative has been kicked off and is underway, the teams will report back to the executive sponsors the issues that require resolution, as well as possibilities for further enhancements that may have a more positive impact on the outcome of the initiative. Executive managers then evaluate and learn from this feedback and pass directives back to the teams, either approving, denying, or amending the teams' recommendations. Your senior managers need to find creative ways to capture and filter this ongoing stream of feedback. This will allow the most brilliant ideas to surface, and they can then either be implemented immediately or become part of the foundation for the next strategic visioning cycle.

This cycle continues throughout the remainder of the project, allowing the project teams to reorganize themselves to tackle new ideas that emerge through this process. Then, when the project is complete and all changes have been transitioned to the greater organization, the recipients of the new order provide ongoing feedback to the executive management team regarding further enhancements, improvements, or modifications, all of which keep the organization in a continuous state of dynamic adaptability and transformation.

The cycle never ceases or rests. The executives learn from the feedback they receive and communicate new directives; the greater organization learns from the new directives, monitors the environment, and provides ongoing feedback to the executives. The ongoing cycle of communication during the implementation of a strategic initiative serves as the final loop that both completes and reinitiates the integrated planning process of the Fifth Ring Strategy, thereby turning the initiative into a self-regulating and self-producing system.

## Continuous Self-Discovery and Renewal

To ensure that your organization is characterized by continuous self-discovery, renewal and transformation you must make the Fifth Ring Strategy as an integral part of the way you do business. Figure 35 models the detailed tasks, integration and flow of an integrated planning process throughout the entire strategic planning and management cycle.

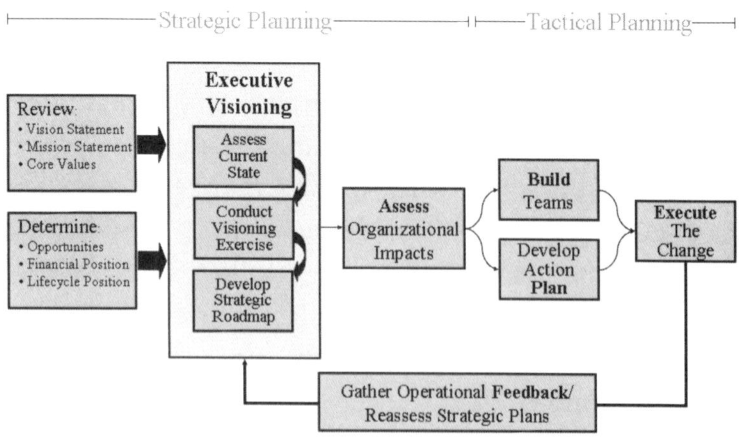


Figure 35. The Flow of the Fifth Ring Strategy

In this model, you can see how foundational information serves as a grounding mechanism for the visioning session, in which your executives review the current state of your company and develop a new strategic roadmap through the strategic visioning process. After the visioning workshop, the new strategic goals and their initiatives are assessed and prioritized. This ends the strategic planning process.

The information that comes out of the strategic planning process is then passed to the selected teams, who plan the detailed actions and execute the new initiatives. Feedback is assessed on an ongoing basis, and the cycle begins once again, either as an annual check-in, or as a visioning retreat to develop an entirely new strategic plan. During key steps along the way, both executives and project team members use the visioning process to foster the emergence of revolutionary ideas that can land your organization on the top of a new peak in the fitness landscape.

If you closely follow the integrated planning process of the Fifth Ring Strategy and rely on its tools and techniques, each member of your organization will develop a communal vision, a collective intention, and a common commitment to achieve the strategic initiative. Your fully aligned organization will work as a single unit to fulfill your organization's strategic goals. If constantly reinforced in the never-ending process of continuous transformation, these three key ingredients for strategic success will likely become a part of your organization's culture.

# Conclusion:

# TRANSCENDING COMPETITION

BY NOW, YOU'VE SEEN how the integrated planning and management process of the Fifth Ring Strategy can allow you to continuously change and transform your organization. During this transformation, you will ultimately be able to shift your focus from the negative aspects of competition to the positive elements of growth and renewal. Miyamoto Musashi's The Book of Five Rings and the Fifth Ring Strategy described in this book are both designed to help you do that.

Competition is not an entity, but rather a frame of mind. Our minds have the ability to create our realities. In other words, if we insist on keeping our minds on competition, that will become our reality. If, on the other hand, we choose to focus our full attention on *becoming* something better by aligning our workforce with a higher purpose and vision, that will, in turn, become our reality.

Just as an example, let's consider the basic family unit, the most common type of organization in the world. Separation and divorce are dividing families at an unprecedented rate. The norm is that both partners work full-time jobs. They come home from a hard day's work and try to relax for a few hours before they have to go to bed. If they don't share a higher common purpose or vision, they grow more and more tired—tired of their work, tired of their relationship, and tired of anything that even resembles routine. But if they have a common higher purpose, a dream, or a shared vision, they have something to aspire towards—something that raises their energy level despite their daily work and routines and chores. They have a dream to chase beyond their daily grind or routine.

If we apply the same principle to our work, we can see that when we think about the same thing day in and day out, we end up with nothing to look forward to. But when we have a common vision and aspire to a higher purpose, we become excited. We know that we have a part in it and that we are growing collectively and individually. We still do our daily operational work, but now we also look forward to the opportunity to create and participate in something exciting and new. This adds value to our lives.

There are two ways to view your organization's attitude toward growth and change. Given the fact that we're all living in the present, or the *here and now*, when you choose to focus on activities that are grounded in fear—fear of failing, fear of losing, fear of not accomplishing—the tendency is to try to preserve what you have and seek stability. Your fears keep you focused on things that happened to you in the past, and you dwell on incidents that previously caused you emotional pain and distress. Perhaps this pain was caused by your company's intolerance of something that failed in the past, or perhaps you lost a major deal with a prized customer. Whatever the case, you're afraid to undergo any kind of change that will again make you vulnerable to such painful emotions. From this attitude, competition is born.

If, on the other hand, you choose to latch on to a higher vision, and make it real by fully visualizing and embodying it in the present, all of your thoughts and actions become aligned with what you are *becoming*, and you will respond much differently. In figure 36 we see the two possible directions you can take from the present. The one is based on fear, the other on vision.

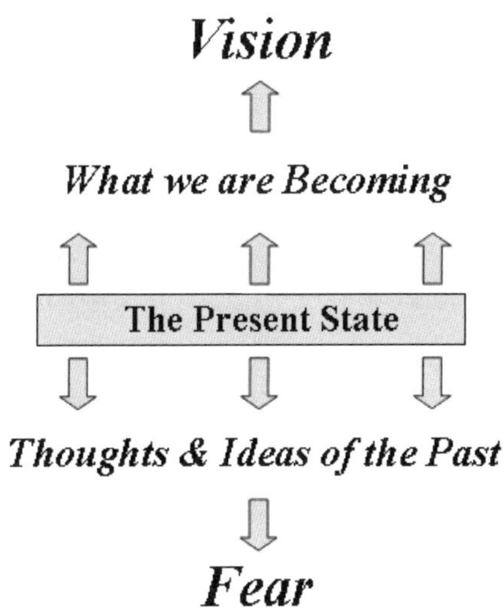


Figure 36. Choices for Directing our Attention

Now let's use this same model to describe how people outside your organization view you. Those who choose to compete with you will direct their attention to what they perceive you to be at the present moment. As competitors, they keep on eye on you out of fear that you may take something from them, be it a new account or some share of the market. This *consciousness of lack* will make your competitors believe that you *are* what you appear to be at that point in time, and they will adjust their strategies to counter your current state. In reality, they only see the manifestation of yesterday's vision.

In the meantime, if your organization is focused on vision and the continuous renewal of your products, your processes, and your people, the competition will have just placed their strategic bets on and committed their resources to nothing more than an illusion. By the time they begin to realize their new strategies, your organization will be revealing the next great idea that can land it on a completely new peak of the competitive landscape.

This simple binary choice of where to focus your attention can either keep you in the heat of battle until you eventually wear down, or it can bring you to a new level, to a *consciousness of abundance* that will free you from the shackling effects of fear. By implementing the Fifth Ring Strategy, you can create an organization focused on change and renewal, one in which all its members share and work toward a common vision, free from the worries of competition. You can either let competition hold you down, or you can transcend it. The choice is yours.

# Appendix

# Musashi's Five Rings of Strategy

IN 1584, MIYAMOTO MUSASHI was born into Japan's Samurai, or warrior, class. Contrary to many stereotypes of this day and age, Musashi was actually a very enlightened soul, and the Samurai played an honorable and significant role in feudal society. They were the epitome of dignity and integrity, and they engaged in battle only to preserve honor and truth. In fact, the word Samurai actually means "those in service." At the tender age of thirteen, Musashi defeated his first opponent, a talented and successful warrior. Using the combined elements of technique, timing, and psychology, Musashi defeated one opponent after the other. By the time he was thirty, he had defeated over sixty opponents. He himself never suffered defeat.

Musashi wasn't just a professional warrior. He was also a talented artist, poet and philosopher who recognized the universal patterns in individual and social behavior as well as in the natural environment. He applied his understanding of these patterns to his art, his philosophy, and his fighting technique, which was both natural and highly effective.

In order to learn all there was to know about his potential opponents, and thus the environment in which he was to operate, Musashi studied and eventually mastered the techniques of all the other *ryu*, or schools of Bushido. He also learned to take advantage of any situation by improvising and using unconventional weapons and techniques, such as practicing on swampy ground using the only tool available to him, which might be just a fence post. He later combined elements of Zen philosophy with his unique fighting techniques to create a new path, or *do,* intended to lead practitioners to a state of enlightenment by shifting the focus from the *battle* to the *winning outcome*.

Musashi's approach can be viewed as a developmental process. As the practitioner learns rings one through four, he finds himself immersed in battle. It isn't until he reaches ring five that he begins to realize the importance of transcending the competitive state. For it is important to first understand the dynamics and strategies of battle, but not to hold such competition-focused ideas as a strategic intention.

Shortly before his death in 1645, Musashi wrote *The Book of Five Rings.* He didn't write the book exclusively for the Samurai. He wanted to make his philosophy available to anyone willing to take the time to learn it. His use of a martial metaphor was simply his way of teaching difficult-to-grasp universal truths by using the easy-to-understand concepts he knew best.

Musashi's book was revolutionary in its time, but it wasn't well known outside of Japan until recently. Although translations can be found in bookstores throughout the Western

Hemisphere, applying his principles in today's business environment can be difficult, especially for those who don't have a background in both organizational strategy and *Bushido*, or the traditional martial arts.

Since we must understand Musashi's principles before we can apply them to modern organizations, I have prepared a paraphrased and synopsized version of *The Book of Five Rings.* In my attempt to make it comprehensible to more people, I have striven to preserve the original meaning of Musashi's message as well as the original context—a feudal Samurai society that was intrinsically competitive and violent. While some passages of Musashi's writings may appear harsh at times to today's reader, it's important to remember that for our purposes, his principles are merely *metaphorical representations* that demonstrate how we can eventually transcend the violent state, or the "heat of battle," and enter the realm of the visionary—for who else would have been better equipped to show us this than Miyamoto Musashi, the master of all Samurai.

As you read, imagine yourself applying the essence of Musashi's principles in your own organization. This will help you identify the obstacles that stand in the way and prepare you to take the foundational steps necessary to achieve the desirable results of the Fifth Ring Strategy.

## Book 1: Earth

Musashi begins by introducing the various disciplines, or occupations, of the era in which he lived—the schools of the Warrior, the Merchant, the Peasant, and the Artisan. He stresses the importance of knowing your own school thoroughly first, and then understanding the importance and principles of all other schools. This is a prerequisite if you, as a practitioner, wish to pursue Musashi's disciplined path, which he called *Heiho*.

Musashi describes the core ideals you are to follow at all times:

- Harbor no sinister thoughts or intentions.
- Pursue this school's discipline diligently.
- Develop a wide range of interests in the arts (i.e., stay creative).
- Develop knowledge of a variety of occupations.
- Practice discretion in everything.
- Nurture the ability to perceive truth in all matters.
- Perceive what cannot be seen with the eye.
- Do not be negligent in even trifling matters.
- Do not engage in useless activity.

Summing up his core ideals, Musashi stresses that you must seek and perceive truth with a broad vision. He adds that if you continuously strive to be physically, mentally, and spiritually strong, you can achieve success in everything you do. Keeping yourself and your subordinates on the path of knowledge, truth, order, and discipline will not only strengthen your position, but also bring honor to your name.

Musashi also addresses the importance of rhythm. While other Samurai schools tended to focus on how to master a single weapon or set of techniques, Musashi's *Heiho* teaches that winning is completely independent of the weapon used. It depends instead on understanding your own rhythm, the rhythm of your opponents, and the rhythm of your surroundings. Musashi stresses that, regardless of the weapon used, understanding the rhythms that take place during battle will enable you to attack using one your opponents don't anticipate, thereby interrupting their sense of timing and ultimately defeating them.

In this book, Musashi uses the earth as a metaphor for the grounding elements of strategy. The values, vision, and knowledge he describes create the foundational elements from which your organization's vision and strategic intentions can unfold and begin to materialize.

## Book 2: Water

In the second book, water is a metaphor for effortless permeation and the ability to maneuver around obstacles while maintaining a conscious state of endless potential that allows you to adapt to any situation at any given time. Here, Musashi highlights the power of conscious awareness, the psychological elements of strategy, and the capacity to remain flexible in whatever direction you choose.

Intention setting is a very important concept in the Book of Water. Without a strong intention, the desired end is subject to random chance. If your opponent holds a stronger intention directed at destroying your strategic intention, you are less likely to achieve yours.

Intention setting doesn't imply that you must plan every detail in advance of a strategic move. Quite the contrary! If you establish an intention—let's say, to deliver the final blow in a competitive engagement—but avoid making detailed plans, you'll have the flexibility to change maneuvers at any time based on the flow of combat.

On the other hand, if you plan each phase prior to a competitive engagement, any unplanned event can disrupt your thinking and leave you in a state of utter confusion. Those who set a higher-level intention while remaining flexible and calm know that they can deploy any number of techniques to achieve the final intention. This gives them a psychological, as well as structural, advantage over those who set intentions at a detailed level and then don't deviate from their plan.

Musashi insists that the body should never pull the mind along. External matters such as size and strength shouldn't concern you as long as your spirit remains strong. And by no means should you reveal the state of your spirit to anyone at any time.

Your mind must remain focused while you're concentrating on any given maneuver. Lack of focus gives your opponent the opportunity to plan his next move. Your mind must stay sharp and concentrated, but your body must remain relaxed. All movements should be natural, continuous, and fluid, with no apparent beginning or end. Continuous fluid movements keep your opponent second-guessing your next move.

While fluidity and flexibility are important elements in the Book of Water, they are futile without a good sense of timing. Timing is the ability to know when to effectively block and counter your opponent's attack. Impeccable timing implies that all the techniques you've learned have become so ingrained that you can instinctively apply them without pausing to think. The transition from one technique to the next should be as fluid as the delivery of each individual technique.

When combined with the grounding elements of the Book of Earth, the principles of intention setting, fluidity, and timing in the Book of Water provide you an effective means of using your core abilities to execute new strategies.

## Book 3: Fire

In the Book of Fire, Musashi focuses on the creative development and execution of strategy. He does so by showing you how to create and master the prerequisite competitive strategies needed to reach an enlightened state in which competition becomes secondary to vision. He exemplifies this creative process through the use of three basic attacks that can be applied at any given time, in any sequence:

1. Strike first: Deliver the deadly blow at the first opportunity.
2. Wait to attack: Allow your opponent to strike first, then act as if the attack had no effect, thus delivering a psychological blow that can cause him to retreat.
3. Counter immediately: Prepare for attack by anticipating what your opponent will do by studying his rhythm, allowing the attack to occur, and then immediately counterattacking.

Musashi goes on to explain that once you understand your opponent's rhythm, or strategy, you should deliver a series of attacks that will break it. Once you've upset your opponent's rhythm, you should keep your momentum going until he collapses. On the other hand, you must also recognize when your opponent has the momentum on his side. In this case, you should quickly withdraw and regroup, thereby preserving yourself to fight in another attack, or even another day.

Musashi provides several examples of applying creative strategy. For example, when you don't know what your opponent's strategy is, you should lead him to believe that you're going to launch a full frontal attack. By initiating the mock attack and then retreating, you can observe how your opponent reacts and often force him to show his hand. By relaxing, you can also mislead him into thinking that you're not prepared to launch an attack. Then, as soon as he attacks, you can execute a quick and decisive countermove. If, on the other hand, your opponent reacts to your perceived state of relaxation by letting down his guard, you can deliver a powerful final blow when he least expects it.

Finally, if you truly know your opponent, you can torment him until you break his concentration and make him react in an emotional fashion. Once he is in an emotional state, you can lead him to act in a way that you've anticipated. This holds true also for armies of opponents. By attacking the corners of their formations using timing and technique superior to their strength in those areas, you can leave them in a state of confusion and fear. Confusion and fear also have rhythms, and if you understand them (by "becoming the enemy") and have good timing, you can lead your opponent to defeat, almost as if his soldiers were your own.

Another strategy Musashi recommends in the Book

of Fire is to emulate a massive rock, thereby making you immovable and impenetrable. You can achieve this by knowing the one formation or technique you can fall back on that will make you virtually impossible to defeat in battle. Knowing this implies that you understand ahead of time both your core strengths and the strengths and weaknesses of your opponent. By having the ability to "become a rock" at any given time or place, you can temporarily retreat and regroup for the next phase of battle. This strategy, while it gives your opponent a chance to regroup and formulate a new strategy, can also wear him down by requiring him to exhaust his resources in a futile attempt to permeate the impermeable.

When you maintain your concentration and creativity at the strategic level of awareness, you will be difficult, if not impossible, to defeat. The strategies of Musashi's third book will enable you to defeat your opponent by pulling his focus and concentration down to a tactical and emotional level. On the other hand, your foundational vision and understanding (Earth), along with strong intention and fluidity (Water), will prepare you to avoid this pitfall yourself.

Once your opponent loses his ability to think strategically, you can easily manipulate him and lead him to defeat. If you do it properly, you can defeat your opponent without the loss of life or limb. Still, this is not an easy task until you have mastered the next book.

## Book 4: Wind

In the Book of Wind, Musashi focuses on knowing your opponent's strengths and weaknesses and the various environments in which a battle can take place. This allows you to make decisive alterations in your strategy unbeknownst to your opponent.

Developing the point he made in the Book of Earth, Musashi describes all of the other schools, or *ryu*, of the Samurai class and points out their distinctive strengths and weaknesses. He stresses the importance of knowing all other schools, or potential opponents, as this knowledge will help you formulate specific, targeted new strategies that you can rapidly modify and execute to catch your opponent off guard.

Musashi then revisits the key elements in the Book of Water. That's because in order to shift strategies rapidly and at will, you need a flexible delivery technique based on the fluidity principles described in that book.

For example, Musashi describes how other schools emphasize specific footwork techniques for different situations. He finds this type of training flawed. He says you need to know all footwork techniques as well as the rhythms an opponent uses to shift from one stance to another. Knowing this allows you to blend the various techniques into one continuous fluid movement that can break your opponent's rhythm, at which time you can effortlessly defeat him. This principle holds true for all types of technique, whether they have to do with footwork, the sword, or general timing.

Musashi says that most schools train their students to keep their focus on their technique. As they shift from technique to technique, so does their focus. He finds this approach fundamentally flawed because if you maintain your focus on one thing, it dampens your spirit. He gives the example of a juggler, who while juggling swords focuses his attention not on the sword being flung in the air, but on the vision of the entire completed act. He focuses on the higher, not the lower. If he were to focus at the lower level of each individual technique or action, he would soon lose his rhythm, thereby placing himself in danger.

You must focus your attention on the overall battle and on the spirit of your opponent, not just his technique. At this level, you will be able to shift and adapt more quickly to his every move and countermove.

Musashi doesn't consider speed a virtue. In fact, he says that speed can be the swiftness or slowness that occurs when your rhythm is off. The techniques of a true master have little, if anything, to do with speed. While these techniques don't always appear to be quick, they do appear to be executed without loss of timing or with any sense of busyness.

Speed is not necessarily undesirable, although it is of little use in certain battle environments, such as a swamp, where the deep mud could make it dangerous. Musashi warns that when an opponent attacks using speedy movements, you shouldn't attempt to match his tempo, but rather stay relaxed and poised, for this could be his strategy to manipulate your rhythm and pull you off guard.

Musashi uses wind as a metaphor for the unpredictable and ever-shifting direction and delivery of your strategy. When you have a deep understanding of your opponent's approach and the ability to deliver different strategies in an unpredictable and fluid manner, you have reached a level of strategic dominance.

Even after you've mastered Earth, Water, Fire, and Wind, continuous exposure to battle or any other form of competition will eventually wear you down and render you ineffective. No one can continue to fight forever. In order to transcend the battle and achieve and maintain a state of enlightened existence, you must eventually master the fifth ring.

## Book 5: Emptiness

Emptiness, or *ku*, is the ultimate state of Musashi's *Heiho*. In fact, all occupational paths in the Zen tradition strive for the enlightened state of emptiness. Emptiness implies the opposite of being filled with "noise," or thoughts that preoccupy the mind, such as the distractions caused by continuous competitive threats. Emptiness ensures our staying in the present, which allows us to focus out attention on that which is right here and right now.

The achievement of emptiness allows us to shift our focus from what "is" to what "is not, yet," or that which "is becoming," unfolding right in front of us. Since nothing ever remains the same, nothing ever "is." No one can ever cross the same river twice, because the flowing water is continually changing. In the same sense, everything is always "becoming." We can achieve this state of awareness only by being and living in the moment, absent of all past- and future-based fears and attachments. In a modern strategic context, this can be a bit confusing. However, if we understand that by practicing strategic visioning (i.e., those techniques discussed in Part III of this book), we are actually observing the desired outcome unfolding in our minds, right here and how. And in doing so, we experience that vision as if it were already happening right in front of us, which enhances our belief and conviction that it can really happen. Through visioning, we actually experience a desired outcome at the cellular level.

Musashi warns us that not every empty state is to be considered *ku*. If you don't strive to fully understand the art of your opponents' school, you can create a dangerous illusion. *Ku* is only *untapped* possibility, or that which is "becoming," or "emerging." An artist sees not only the objects painted on the canvas, but also, and more importantly, what is not on the canvas—the empty spaces that contain infinite possibility. An artist must first fully comprehend what *is* on the canvas, then discern from it what *is not*. Musashi claims that your spirit can be pure only when, like the artist, you live in the moment, recognize the continuity of change, and seize the opportunities offered by each transition.

Musashi also says that nothing has meaning in and of itself. An object begins to acquire meaning only when it is recognized in relationship to other things. For example, an apple by itself has no meaning if there's no one who holds an intention for it (e.g. to eat it). Therefore, we can say that all that exists does so only in relation to other things.

This is important because any vision you have has no meaning unless there's a context in which you can apply it. Recognizing the cause-and-effect relationships within your personal realm of experience and expertise allows you to weed out visions that aren't useful. Then you can focus on the ones that are most applicable in any given situation.

What does all this mean for you as a practitioner of

Musashi's *Heiho*? It means that you can be successful in battle for a long time by practicing the principles of rings one through four. But it also means that you will be able to endure a continuous state of engagement with and focus on the opponent for only so long before you begin to break down.

Even if you don't break down first, your opponent will surely begin to recognize and understand the patterns of your competitive strategy and ultimately defeat you. If, on the other hand, you stay focused on the continuous renewal of your vision by training your mind to focus on what is "becoming"—the opportunity offered at any given moment—a refreshing, continuous rebirth of thought will replace the pressure of competitive battle. You will step out of the circle of fear and focus solely on continuous self-renewal and self-actualization.

What does this mean for your opponents? Your mastery of the art of Emptiness will leave them second-guessing your every move without ever being able to formulate their own proactive strategy. Through an infinite source of new ideas and strategies, you will lead them to the conclusion that you are an entity to avoid, and not fight.

Ultimately, as a master practitioner who has achieved the state of Emptiness, you and your workforce will transcend the state of continuous challenge and competition. You will find yourself living more creatively—continuously regenerating new ideas and vision that most of your opponents will either hopelessly challenge, or, more likely, completely avoid. In the Empty state you are in a class of your own, in which you are primarily focused on your own sense of vision and self-discovery.

Times have certainly changed since the day of the Samurai warrior. Most people no longer roam the countryside testing new methods by which they can more effectively cut other people to pieces. This is a good thing!

Nevertheless, when applied metaphorically to the strategic issues with which many organizations now struggle, the principles of Musashi's five rings can be just as effective and applicable today as they were back then.

# Bibliography

Argyris, Chris. "Teaching Smart People How to Learn." *Harvard Business Review* (May/June 1991): 99–109.

Argyris, Chris, and Donald Schon. *Organizational Learning: A Theory of Action Perspective.* Reading, MA: Addison-Wesley, 1978.

________. *Theory in Practice: Increasing Professional Effectiveness.* San Francisco: Jossey-Bass, 1992.

Barabasi, Albert L. *Linked.* New York: Penguin Plume, 2003.

Beniger, James R. *The Control Revolution: Technological and Economic Origins of the Information Society.* Cambridge, MA: Harvard University Press, 1986.

Blank, Renee, and Sandra Slipp. *Voices of Diversity.* New York: AMACOM, 1994.

Burns, Tom, and G. M. Stalker. "Mechanistic and Organic Systems." *Classics of Organization Theory,* 4th ed. J. M. Shafritz and J. S. Ott, eds. Orlando, FL: Harcourt Brace, 1996.

Bushnell, Don, Keith Bergthold, and Niels Agger-Gupta. "Building Social Capital and Organizational Capacity in Community-Based Nonprofit Organizations through Appreciative Inquiry." *OD Practitioner,* 34, no. 4 (2002): 14–19.

Capra, Fritjof. *The Turning Point: Science, Society and the Rising Culture.* New York: Bantam Books, 1982.

Castells, Manuel *The Rise of the Network Society.* Malden, MA: Blackwell Publishers, 1996.

Collins, James, and Jerry Porras. *Built to Last.* New York: Harper Business Books, 1997.

Cooperider, David L., and Diana Whitney. *Collaborating for Change: Appreciative Inquiry*. San Francisco: Berret-Koehler, 2000.

Daneke, Gregory. "Coming Full Circle: On the Return of Systems Thinking to Strategic Management." *Journal of Business and Management* (Fall 1994): 8–33.

________. *Systemic Choices: Nonlinear Dynamics and Practical Management*. Ann Arbor: University of Michigan Press, 1999.

Donaldson, Gordon. *Managing Corporate Wealth: The Operation of a Comprehensive Financial Goals System*. New York: Praeger, 1984.

Drucker, Peter. "Long Range Planning." *Management Science* 5 (1959): 3.

Gardner, Howard. *Multiple Intelligences: The Theory in Practice.* New York: Basic Books, 1993.

Gleick, James *Chaos: Making a New Science.* New York: Penguin Books, 1987.

Hamel, Gary *Leading the Revolution*. Boston, MA: Harvard Business School Press, 2000.

Handy, Charles. *The Hungry Spirit.* New York: Broadway Books, 1998.

Harvey, Jerry B. *The Abilene Paradox: The Management of Agreement.* New York: AMACOM, 1974.

Heim, Matthew C. "Business Leaders Evaluate the Systemic Planning Process: Four Organizations' Experiences." Santa Barbara, CA: A Published Dissertation Abstract of the Fielding Graduate Institute, 2002.

Hendricks, Gay, and Kate Ludeman. *The Corporate Mystic: A Guidebook for Visionaries with their Feet on the Ground.* New York: Bantam Books, 1996.

Hurst, David K., and Zimmerman, Brenda J. "From Lifecycle to Ecocycle." *Journal of Management Inquiry* 3, no. 4 (December 1994): 339–354.

Jaworski, Joseph *Synchronicity: The Inner Path of Leadership.* San Francisco: Barrett Koehler, 1996.

Katzenbach, Jon R., and Douglas K. Smith. *The Wisdom of Teams: Creating the High-Performance Organization.* New York: Harper Perennial, 1999.

Kotter, John P. *A Force for Change: How Leadership Differs From Management.* New York: The Free Press, 1990.

________. *Leading Change.* Boston, MA: Harvard Business School Press, 1996.

Kuhn, Thomas S. *The Structure of Scientific Revolutions.* Chicago, IL: University of Chicago Press, 1970.

Mingers, John. *Self-Producing Systems: Implications and Applications of Autopoiesis.* New York: Plenum, 1995.

Musashi, Miyamoto. *The Book of Five Rings.* New York: Bantam Books, 1982.

Negroponte, Nicholas P. *Being Digital.* New York: Vintage Books, 1995.

Oshry, Barry *Seeing Systems: Unlocking the Mysteries of Organizational Life.* San Francisco: Barrett Koehler, 1995.

Pascale, Richard T., Mark Millemann, and Linda Gioja. *Surfing the Edge of Chaos.* New York: Crown, 2000.

Porter, Michael E. *Competitive Strategy.* New York: The Free Press, 1980.

________. *Competitive Advantage: Creating and Sustaining Superior Performance*. New York: The Free Press, 1985.

Rumelt, Richard P., Dan E. Schendel, and David J. Teece. *Fundamental Issues in Strategy*. Boston, MA: Harvard Business School Press, 1994.

Senge, Peter M. *The Fifth Discipline: The Art and Practice of the Learning Organization.* New York: Currency Doubleday, 1990.

Shapiro, Carl, and Hal R.Varian. *Information Rules.* Boston, MA: Harvard Business School Press, 1999.

Stacey, Ralph *Complexity and Creativity in Organizations.* San Francisco: Berrett-Koehler, 1996.

Tart, Charles T. *States of Consciousness.* Lincoln, NE: Back-inprint.com, 2001.

Teece, David "Economic Analysis and Strategic Management." Glenn R. Carrol and David Vogel, eds. *Strategy and Organization: A West Coast Perspective.* Boston MA: Pittman, 1984.

Thomas R. Roosevelt Jr. *Beyond Race and Gender.* New York: AMACOM, 1991.

Tichy, Noel M., and Eli Cohen. "The Teaching Organization." *Training and Development* (July 1998): 27–33.

Wheatley, Margaret. *Leadership and the New Science.* San Francisco: Berrett-Koehler Publishers, 1951.

Willard, Bob *The Sustainability Advantage: Seven Bottom Line Benefits of a Triple Bottom Line.* BC, Canada: New Society Publishers, 2002.

Williams, Garnett P. *Chaos Theory Tamed.* Washington, DC: Joseph Henry Press, 1997.

Youngblood, Mark D. *Life at the Edge of Chaos: Creating the Quantum Organization.* Dallas, TX: Perceval Publishing, 1997.

# Index